GET
PUBLISHED

INDUSTRY EXPERTS SHARE THEIR SECRETS

ISBN: 979-8-9872110-1-4

Cover design by Kristina Conatser, capturedbykcdesigns.com
Edited by Dragonfly De La Luz, dragonflyediting.com
Social Media Graphics by Meagan Caesar, meagecaesar.com
Book design by James Woosley, freeagentpress.com

We're happy to announce that the launch proceeds of
Get Published: Industry Experts Share Their Secrets
will go to an organization that is
near and dear to our hearts, Elimu Girls.

Elimu Girls is a 501(c)(3) organization that empowers rural Kenyan teens to become entrepreneurs, ensuring financial freedom, self-worth, and equality.

Upon graduation from their two-year sewing
and boarding program, the girls will have
a voice, a choice, and a bank account.

Find out more about Elimu Girls at elimugirls.com.

EDITOR'S NOTE:

Out of respect for the global origins of our international contributors, some chapters adhere to American grammatical conventions regarding spelling, quotes, and initials, while others reflect British standards.

Contents

Introduction

You may tell a tale that takes up residence in someone's soul, becomes their blood, and self, and purpose.

—Erin Morgenstern

You have a desire that has likely been burning for quite some time to write and publish a book, a treasured dream that is held by so many, yet realized by so few. Now you're finally ready to excavate this idea from your heart to fruition. Congratulations! Just by picking up this book and flirting with the idea of sharing your message, story, wisdom, or expertise with the world, you're announcing to the Universe loud and clear that you're ready to be supported in this endeavor. By clearing away the excuses, limiting beliefs, and hurdles of the past, you're making way for a clearly defined and deeply supported path toward authorship to materialize. You're making room in your life to birth something new.

As you step into making this dream a reality, it is paramount to give it the reverence and time it deserves.

After my youngest daughter was born, I rushed back to work too soon, convinced that if I could prove to my employer that I could work two weeks postpartum after a cesarean, they would surely let me work from home a couple days a week. They eventually did, but the high price I had to pay for that arrangement was a sacrifice. What should have been extra time snuggling my baby was instead more time I spent being pulled in too many directions—paperwork in one hand, a baby in the other, my 10-year-old desperate for attention, and my 2-year-old pleading with me to put down the baby so she could sit on my lap. I felt desperate and wasn't able to give any of them the attention they deserved, especially that baby. It still breaks my heart just thinking about it. And because I was so spread thin, I ended up making a big mistake that almost cost the company I was working for thousands of dollars. We fixed it, but it was a close call.

If you've ever tried to pile too much into an already full schedule and ended up sacrificing what was most important, then you know what I'm talking about. Now, even though my baby-making days are over, anytime I start something new, whether it's a book, exercise regimen, project I'm working on, or course I'm taking, I make sure to carve out the time and space so that this "new baby" is cared for and I enjoy the time I spend doing it. Otherwise, that important thing I'd be sacrificing would be… me.

Writing a book, whether it's a chapter in a multiauthor book like this one, a 40,000-word manuscript, or working with a ghostwriter to tell your story, is going to need your loving care and attention. You can try to cram it into an overbooked life, or you can clear out some space and give it the time that it—and you—deserve.

Having said that, writing a book requires more than just time and space. It requires commitment. How many times have you started something and not finished it? You were super excited with the idea of it but ended up letting it fall by the wayside. Although it's impossible to know for sure, some online sources say that an astonishing 97 percent of people who start writing a book never finish. If that's true, I want you to know that the other 3 percent, the ones who follow their dreams all the way to their fruition, are no different than you or me. They don't necessarily have more money or more time. The only thing that sets them apart is what they commit to, what they choose to do with that time.

Think about the last time you showed up consistently and worked towards a goal. Whether it was a college degree, a home improvement project, or that smoking-hot body you worked so hard for, it likely didn't happen overnight. There is magic in the mundane; it was the small, consistent steps you took every day that made accomplishing those goals possible. You didn't start seeing results until you had dedicated yourself to working at it for quite some time. Right when you started to get really exhausted, you pushed yourself just a little farther, and that's how you got past the finish line.

Feeling so tired you don't know if you can do it anymore, or being so overwhelmed you want to gouge your eyes out, is actually a sign that you're almost there. Unfortunately, that's where most people stop. They don't have the staying power to sit through that discomfort or the wherewithal to seek guidance. And that's when a lot of manuscripts die. But you're not "most people." I want you to be in that 3 percent, the ones who look at all the priorities in their life vying for attention and decide, perhaps for the very first time, to prioritize committing to their own dreams.

Once you commit to doing something, do it—and see your life change. Whether it's a commitment to yourself *(I'm going to write for one hour each day)* or a commitment to someone else *(I'll be at that party you're hosting)*, unless something unforeseen prevents you from doing it, make it happen. That's where you start to build trust in yourself and train your subconscious mind that you are capable of following through with your commitments, even on days you don't want to. That's where you show those around you what you stand for. That's where you begin to stand for you.

You did say you were going to read this book from start to finish, right? Well, there you go. Let's start there and follow through with that small commitment. Besides, you wouldn't want to miss out on all the nuggets of wisdom waiting for you here.

It's likely that this won't be the first time you've heard some of the insights, ideas, concepts, and tools shared inside this book. But I encourage you to approach it with the curiosity of a child.

My 9-year-old daughter, McKenzie, loves the Reborn baby dolls. You know the ones that look eerily like actual babies? Each time she gets a new one, she becomes consumed with it. She carves out a space for it to stay in, she carefully selects the best outfits, and she's mesmerized by the uniqueness of this particular baby doll as if it's the first time she's ever seen one.

Are you willing to approach this book with similar care and curiosity? Create a space for this version of ideas to come through. Some of our experts have put a new spin on classic concepts. Allow yourself to embark on this journey with fresh eyes, and this book will guide you deeper into wisdom and to higher heights of inspiration.

You are not the same person you were one year ago, one month ago, or even last week. I encourage you to engage this book accordingly, meeting these ideas from where you are right now and letting them carry you toward new revelations. Your inner wisdom already knows what messages you are meant to take away from this book.

Books are mirrors: You only see in them what you already have inside you.

—Carlos Ruiz Zafón

The insights from the experts shared inside this book are unique to their own perspectives and expertise. The combination of who they are, their experiences, and the lens through which they have perceived their experiences has perfectly positioned them to deliver the messages within these pages. Are you ready to receive? Trust that whatever you're meant to glean from this book will highlight with clarity your next steps.

Different chapters might resonate with you in different ways throughout your writing and publishing journey. Today, you might be inspired by knowledge offered in one chapter, while next month a concept from another chapter might resonate. Like any good book, I encourage you to revisit this one often.

Whether it's setting time aside to read this book, making an intention to implement the lessons you've learned from it, or fully committing to getting your work published this year, taking action is a necessary and dynamic step in fulfilling your goals. That could mean reaching out to one of the experts in this book for a consultation or taking what you've learned and making the journey on your own. Whatever the case, *take action.*

The one thing I hope you take away from this book is that regardless of where you are on your path to authorship, you are so supported. There are legions of ancestors that rejoiced the moment you picked up this book, elated that you are taking steps to make your publishing dreams come true. The entire Universe supports those who make the sacred choice to commit to their dreams. Every expert in this book, though they may never know your name, is supporting you in ways you cannot see, but will surely feel through the words in these pages.

Something is calling to be expressed through you, in a way that only you can actualize. Leaving this legacy, putting your unique stamp on the world that contributes to the wisdom and knowledge of the collective, is both an honor and a duty. Carry that responsibility with joy and reverence.

Roll up your sleeves and let's get writing.

Chapter 1

Let Your Wisdom Outlive Your Life

by Krystal Hille

If you listen real close, you can hear them whisper their legacy to you. Go on, lean in... Carpe diem, seize the day... Make your lives extraordinary.

—Robin Williams, in *Dead Poets Society*

It was an afternoon like any other. I was sitting at my desk, briefly scrolling Facebook, when I got stopped in my tracks. I saw a post commemorating one of my VIP clients. Wait, what? We had just completed developmental edits for her chapter. I held my breath, staring at the computer screen in utter disbelief. Yes, I'd read correctly. She'd passed away unexpectedly from a heart attack. I could still hear her

German-accented voice sharing her passion to bridge cultural segregation. Being a German expat myself, we often spoke in both languages and had grown quite close. Suddenly, I felt a huge responsibility at the realisation that I had been entrusted with her legacy—quite literally.

The reason I'm telling you this story is because you never know when your time is up. There is only this now-moment. If you were to leave this world tomorrow, could you look back saying, 'Yes, I've lived full out'? 'Yes, I've seized the day'? 'Yes, I contributed to the world in a meaningful way and realised my calling to publish my wisdom in a book'? Don't leave it on your bucket list!

According to a survey referenced in the *New York Times* in 2002, 81 percent of respondents believe they should write a book. 'Someday', right? Or perhaps you're that person who's written an entire draft of a book that takes up space on your desktop or gathers dust in reams of notebooks. Why don't more people follow through with their writing dreams? Well, I can think of a few reasons: We're scared. We don't have time. We don't know how. We've all heard, or even used, the usual excuses:

I'll get around to it someday.

It's just not the right time now.

I'm too busy.

The truth is, it's never the right time to write a book, just like it's never the right time to have a baby. But there comes a day when you're done playing small and ready to make a decision that will change your life. There is always magic beyond our comfort zone, *always*. And just as certainly, there will be blocks that keep you from getting there.

What if my writing sucks?

You don't have to be a writer to be an author. Really, you don't! All you need is a passion for your story and the desire to share your wisdom. A good publisher will make you look good (and there are many voice-to-text apps that can help you get your initial ideas down with ease).

What will my family and high school friends think? Who do I think I am, anyway?

If you're suffering from imposter syndrome, you are not alone. I've helped many of my clients overcome this dilemma by transforming their self-doubt into self-confidence, so they step fully into owning their hard-earned wisdom and sharing it fearlessly.

My story is far too edgy and vulnerable.

Vulnerability is the key that opens the door to your reader's heart. Stories connect us. Without sharing your challenges, you're unrelatable, and no one will care about your successes.

> *I write so you know you are not alone. I stand in*
> *vulnerability so that you know it's okay for you to stand*
> *in yours.*
>
> —Haben Delalatta,
> contributing author of *Inspired Living*

These blocks are real, but if your soul whispers for you to publish your work and you let fear or circumstances get in the way, you are selfish. Why? Because you are a unique expression of the divine, and your life is the Universe itself speaking through you to impact others. Your story is the only unique thing you've got. No one shares it, nor your perspective, nor your exquisite combination of talents. Just like no one shares your fingerprint.

Make your experiences count, so your pain will not be in vain. Not only has pain in some way enriched your life, but your hindsight can now provide hope and inspiration to those going through similar difficulties. Publishing your story lets your message live beyond your life.

That's what I'm passionate about! As a publisher who creates collaborative books, I weave a web of wayshowers together. I gather purpose-led entrepreneurs and divine feminine leaders who hold an empowered vision and high frequency for the planet. I am committed to educating, enriching, empowering, inspiring, and activating humans across all nations to strengthen their belief in themselves, to transform their lives so they can be the creators of their destinies.

Together, we offer readers inspiration, hope, and tools to transform their pain and ultimately raise the frequency of humanity. My intention is to create books that contribute to the awakening and empowerment of humanity, so that we may all come into deeper sovereignty and connection during this time of great planetary transition.

Let me unpack this.

Awaken. We need to release life on autopilot and remember that we are not our emotions, so that we become the observer and recognise the cultural and familial context that has created our beliefs, patterns, and behaviours.

Empower. It requires courage to take life into our own hands and leave the familiar but dysfunctional world behind so that we can create one that aligns with our true essence.

Sovereignty. The Asch experiments of the 1950s showed that we would rather be knowingly wrong in a group in order to belong, than be right and stand alone. We've been conditioned to live in fear of our power so that we stay dependent on a system, tribe, teacher, or romantic relationship. When we learn to fully love ourselves and deepen into self-trust, we can disentangle from all codependent relationships.

Connection. As humans, we crave connection. It is essential for our survival. I imagine a world that celebrates, not crushes, uniqueness, whilst embracing the power of community and collaboration. And through my publishing house, I am creating that world.

Dr. John Demartini says, 'Our voids create our values'. This is certainly true for me. As a child, I wasn't empowered. In fact, I believe that I recreated circumstances from past lives to resolve the many forms of disempowerment throughout my lifetimes, all the way back to Atlantis. That's not a mission for the faint-hearted; it's one thing to know that we are strong, but it's quite another to call on that strength for survival and release the shackles of inner and outer control.

I grew up in the safety of a church minister's family, with noble values, beautiful rituals, stories, art, and mythology. Life was good until a life-changing accident at age four, when my baby brother kicked boiling hot water over my chest. I ended up in hospital for 10 days, naked and in isolation. Though horrifying, this accident was necessary to activate memories of past slavery to dissolve disempowerment. That undertaking has turned out to be a decades-long process.

I never dreamt that the tumult I faced in my forties was even possible. I entered many cycles of people-pleasing, perfectionism, and seeking external validation. I created repeated situations proving how disempowered I really was, culminating in my recent divorce and a brain tumour diagnosis. (I survived, surgery was successful, and I'm here to tell the tale. But that's another story for another book.)

Although the last two years have been tough, leading me to become intimately familiar with anxiety, I now can say I have finally reclaimed my strength, my power, an unshakeable belief in myself, and trust in higher guidance. What I've been through has ignited a fire in my belly to help others identify the red flags of codependency, narcissism, gaslighting, and guru abuse *before* they get sucked into situations that will cause upheaval in their lives.

One reader at a time, we're healing ancestral wounds and putting an end to filling inner voids with people-pleasing, perfectionism, control, and other addictive behaviours that make us either victims or perpetrators in codependent relationships. Imagine a world where connection can once again come from a place of empowerment, not neediness!

Empowerment has been the throughline in all my careers. It started when I was a theatre director and drama teacher. I empowered actors to give their best performance and was once complimented by an in-house teacher that I have a gift of bringing the personality of each actor into the character they embody. I believe this is because being a Scorpio with extrasensory abilities helps me to truly *see* people. I see your potential, and when I reflect it back to you, it gives you the ability to embody it in a deeper way and express it, be that on stage or in writing.

As a publisher, I provide platforms for influencers and role models to share the ways of a new paradigm, so that our children and grandchildren can live in peace, prosperity, and freedom. And as an activator of transformation, I facilitate coaching sessions to empower my clients to return to self-trust and wholeness—just as I did when I decided to embark on this journey of becoming an indie publisher.

It was January 2021, during the pandemic. I sat at my large mahogany desk, staring out the window after reviewing local job adverts, when I suddenly realised… I'm unemployable! I was either overqualified or underqualified for anything on the marketplace.

Always following my passions, I'd never worked a corporate job. My twenties saw me touring Europe as a theatre director and drama teacher. In my thirties, I became a transformational coach, and in my forties, a tantra teacher and facilitator. The pandemic closed all my workshops and temple nights. I had just one client in my coaching practice, probably because after leaving my husband, I was barely able to hold space for myself and my kids, let alone anyone else. I'd hoped to just buckle down and get a stable job until I could get out of the quicksand, but that was obviously not what the Universe had in mind for me.

I've always had a firm belief in higher guidance, and throughout my life I've trusted synchronicities above reason. For example, moving from the UK to Australia was based on this trust, as was leaving an ex-boyfriend despite the possibility of deportation. The Universe always rewards the brave, and the harder the decisions have been, the more rewarding the magic that awaited me on the other side. This time was no different.

Having been in four anthologies previously, I remembered the publisher offered publishing training. This resonated deeply, even though it didn't make sense. I felt a full-body, shivers-down-the-spine, *Yes!* while my mind was playing the catch-up game, puzzled about how a publisher could awaken and empower humanity. Turns out, it was on point in more ways than I could have imagined. Writing is transformational. And in the words of Robin Williams, 'No matter what anybody tells you, words and ideas can change the world'.

With my back against the wall and this publishing opportunity my only lifeline, I had to make it work. And so I did. In February 2021, I founded Hille House Publishing, an indie publishing house specialising in multiauthor and solo books in the personal development and spiritual growth genres, with a particular passion for books that educate, activate, and inspire readers who have been in codependent relationships or experienced narcissism, gaslighting, guru abuse, or spiritual slavery.

In less than two years, we have worked with 144 contributors from 26 countries and published six No. 1 international bestsellers in at least three to five countries, with two more in the making and a further four in the planning phase in collaboration with other organisations. As I said, the Universe rewards courage! We have attracted the likes of Dr.

John Demartini, Dr. Larry Farwell, and Lorie Ladd as lead authors, giving other contributing authors added authority by association.

HOW CONTRIBUTING TO A MULTIAUTHOR BOOK TRANSFORMS THE AUTHOR

Being all about empowerment, what lights me up most is the transformation the authors undergo in the writing process and the opportunities they receive from our work together. Take Keen Nichols, for example, a co-author of *Inspired Living* who has just completed his very own summit and fully claimed his niche in shadow work. He told me that this would not have been possible without joining our *Inspired Living* book. I remember him asking me all the tough questions, which essentially boiled down to, 'Do you really care about me? Do you really know what you're doing, or do you just want my money'? His heart already knew the answer. It resonated with my soul. He soon understood that contributing to this collaborative book was about so much more than becoming an international No. 1 bestselling author to increase his expert status and visibility. It was about deepening the embodiment of his message, claiming his expertise, and coming out with his backstory that had been the cause of deep shame for many years.

There have been so many more contributors who released shame in the process of writing, opening them up to more life force, radiance, and magnetism.

> *Wow, that's so exciting and liberating. I feel like any tiny bit of shame regarding my story that may have been left released after writing. It's out there for the world to see now! No more hiding and not being seen or heard.*
>
> —Niki Woods,
> contributing author of *Intuitive Living*

This is not surprising, because according to David R. Hawkins's map of consciousness, shame vibrates at the lowest frequency of 20Hz, compared to unconditional love, which vibrates at 528Hz. From a place of love, it's easier to listen to and act on the whispers of our soul: *Carpe diem! Organise a summit. Write your solo book. Create a high-ticket retreat with another contributor. Expand, expand, expand!*

I'm convinced that contributing to a multiauthor book or writing your solo book with the right publisher is also the most effective way to get to your next level of personal exposure and expansion from where you can attract more soul-aligned clients.

Books solve a visibility problem. They give you better positioning in the marketplace by elevating your authority status, which offers you the opportunity to not only raise your prices, but attract greater media attention, giving you more exposure to future clients.

Writing a book is also a deeply transformational experience, especially in my containers, which have been specifically designed to facilitate personal growth for professional expansion.

Underpinning all the above reasons to write your book is the opportunity to leave a legacy and make a difference for future generations.

> *Deepest heartfelt gratitude to you, Krystal, because this has been one of my dreams. It's been in my vortex for a long time to write a book, and you just have made one of my dreams come true. And it has unfolded with such ease.*
> —Emma Grey,
> contributing author of *Inspired Living*

If you are a purpose-led entrepreneur, divine feminine leader, coach, consultant, or professional with wisdom that you don't want to take into your grave, then one of our programs, where we take you by the hand and provide step-by-step systems and strategies that make the process of writing easy, may just be right for you. I share more about the different offers we have in the Work with Us section of this book.

I have developed a profound understanding of humanity as well as a sensitivity for cultures (having lived in four different countries and visited many more), coupled with life experiences that have given me buckets of humility and compassion for the human condition. My high-level systems and professionalism are underpinned by a deeply intuitive awareness and extrasensory abilities. I'm in my happy place when I can explore the depth of my clients' soul journey and the insights they have gained, and ensure that their message translates onto the page.

Writing is a practice. Whether you want to write your book, contribute a chapter to an anthology, or become better at writing blog posts, start writing every day for just five to 10 minutes and do so as fast as you can without stopping. This will help you to empty your brain, bypass the conscious mind, and access your deeper wisdom with less effort.

I believe that writing is more than just putting words on paper. It's a portal to our inner selves and the universe around us. When I write, time stops, and I'm transported to a different realm where I'm connected with the creative potential of the universe and the mystery of my being.

Having said all of that, remember that you don't have to be a writer to be an author. What's important is your intention and desire to share your wisdom. As Maya Angelou says, 'There is no greater agony than bearing an untold story inside of you'.

In closing, I would like you to imagine that exciting moment when you open the parcel and hold your book for the very first time. As you flick through the pages, the fragrance of this fresh-off-the-press book tickles your nostrils, and you feel pride spreading into your whole body. You see yourself jumping into the air in sheer joy, telling yourself, *I've done it. I've done it!*

You're proud that you've seized the day, grateful that you've paid attention to the whispers of your soul, and thrilled that you've made a decision and taken courageous action. Now magic and infinite possibilities await you.

Seize the day!

ABOUT THE AUTHOR

Krystal Hille is the founder of Hille House Publishing, a Soul Leadership coach, speaker, and multiple international No. 1 bestselling author.

In the past two years, Krystal has helped around 150 changemakers from 26 countries to become international bestselling authors so that their passion can ignite global change and enhance their authority and reach. She has attracted lead authors such as Dr. John Demartini, Dr. Larry Farwell, and Lorie Ladd.

With 30 years in leadership, a BA (Hons) in English, and a background in theatre-directing, ancient tantric practices, transformational coaching, NLP, healing, and female empowerment, she is passionate about gathering changemakers who align with her mission to awaken and empower humanity.

Krystal is a winner of the CREA Brainz Global Business Award 2021 and runner-up in the Regional Victorian Awards for Innovation and Leadership. Aware of her multidimensional self, Krystal has facilitated spiritual retreats to Egypt and run temple nights across Australia.

Originally from Germany, Krystal currently lives in country Victoria, Australia, with her two children.

Connect with Krystal:
- ➤ Website: krystalhille.org
- ➤ Linktree: linktr.ee/krystalhille
- ➤ Take the Author Archetype Quiz: krystalhille.org/author-archetype-quiz

Chapter 2

If Not Now, When?

by Larissa Soehn

So many people have the goal of writing a book, yet only a very small percentage actually do. "Why is that?" you might ask. The answer may surprise you. It's not because writing a book is hard. It's not because you need to be a natural-born writer. And it certainly isn't because you don't have the time. It's because the idea of writing a book is overwhelming. People quit before they even start because the *idea* is so scary that they don't even try. That's where I come in.

Let's rewind a bit to my first book, a science-fiction novel. When I started writing, I had no idea what I was writing about. I didn't even know I was writing a book. I was not one of the throngs of people that had a goal of writing a book. It happened accidentally, and I think that was one of the biggest factors in my success. I didn't know what I was doing, which meant I didn't lose sleep over the idea. There were no moments of being overwhelmed. There were no thoughts of dread or imposter syndrome. I simply fell into the writing and let it take over.

This wasn't just a one-time thing, either. I was able to "fall" into writing many more times over the years, but let's jump forward to when I purposefully set out to write a book.

WRITING WITH INTENTION

When I started my coaching business, I knew I would need to write a book to showcase what I did and make it easy and accessible for people. Stepping into the coaching world for me was like answering a call that had been ignored for a long time. I knew I was meant to connect with people on a deeper level than what my corporate position was offering me. I also learned very quickly that I would never be able to serve all those that needed me. This is where my book came in.

As if starting a business wasn't complicated enough, I piled the idea of writing a book on top of it. I launched the business in late October, and in early December, I launched my international bestselling book. It took me 10 weeks to write, edit, market, and publish a bestselling book that would ultimately boost my business. It was short and sweet, sitting at about 30,000 words with pages used up for workbook space, and yet it was my most challenging project simply because I let the idea get to me.

So, let's talk about what it means to have an idea. An idea is the conceptualization of a new reality, or at least that's my definition of it. It's when our minds come up with something that is going to change the way we see our world, whether it be through the way we act, think, or behave. Nothing starts without an idea, books included. Now, I know that I said earlier that my first book started accidentally, without an idea, but that isn't completely true. It started with the idea that I needed a creative outlet to escape my reality for a bit, and this seemed like the best avenue. The idea wasn't, *I'm going to write a 90,000-word book.* It was, *I'm going to write for a while and see where it takes me.*

When I look back on the difference in mindset between my first book and my business-boosting book, I see a stark difference in the approach. The first book was casual while the business book was formal, and my mindset felt the shift.

So, this is my message to you: Don't let the idea of writing a book overwhelm you to the point that you never start. For some, you might have the idea of a story sitting in your mind, while others simply have the goal of writing a book. Regardless of where you are right now, as a book coach, I highly recommend you let the goal of writing a book go and think of it in smaller terms. Again, the idea of writing a book is what stops the majority of people from even starting, much less finishing.

Here are some alternative ideas to the overwhelming thought of writing a book:

I'm going to make it part of my daily routine to write for an hour. Adding a habit into your life, especially one that is proven to be incredibly healthy for our emotional and mental well-being, is an amazing goal to have. What happens in that hour each day is left up to you in the moment.

I'm going to tell a story. For many of us, stories are for children. They are short and simple. By telling yourself that you are simply setting out to tell a story, you're signaling to your mind that what you are about to do will be simple. There are no overwhelming feelings or moments of dread. This simple change in verbiage can make all the difference in your motivation.

I need a break from this busy world and writing will be my escape. Sometimes we forget why it is that we are writing. We can get lost in the idea that we are writing because we have to. That is rarely the case. By switching the narrative to something that by nature is more beneficial to you and your health, you will instinctively be more inclined to do it. Consider the moment when life gets crazy and you really need a break. Why not turn to writing? It's scientifically proven to reduce stress and anxiety, according to a 2018 study published in the *British Journal of Health Psychology*. After just 10 minutes, your body and mind will have quieted down and you will be in a new state.

As a coach that specializes in helping coaches write books to boost their business, I know exactly what mental barriers people are up against when it comes to starting their books. In fact, the biggest barrier to getting clients in the first place is the mentality that says, "Not now, but in the future." The people that say this are part of the group that never write their book.

My biggest question to these people is, "If not now, when?"

Whenever we've started something new, was the moment ever perfectly right? Did we have an abundance of time, money, or support? Did we know the outcome would be perfect? No. Absolutely not. But we did it anyway. We took a leap and dared to do something great. That is what writing a book is all about. There are a million reasons why now is not the time, but there are a million-and-one reasons that make now the perfect time.

Consider this for a moment: You are a burned-out entrepreneur, mother, and wife. Life is absolutely bonkers and there is no end in sight, despite the fact that you keep telling yourself things will get easier. I'm here to tell you that "easy" doesn't just happen. You have to work for easy. You have to change and grow if you want your life to do the same. There will never be a perfect time for us to grow. There will never be a serendipitous moment when the stars align and everything is exactly the way it needs to be. But I beg that you don't let that stop you.

THE SECRET BENEFITS OF WRITING A BOOK

Writing a book is like giving birth to a child. When you choose to do it, there is extreme joy associated with it, and extreme pain. The world was never perfectly ready for their arrival. That doesn't mean the child should never have been; it only means that we adapted to their needs and made ourselves available. Basically, we did what had to be done.

Just like a child, your book will come packed with benefits you may not have anticipated. Let's talk for a moment about what those benefits can do for you and your business, because sometimes we get lost in the glamour and overlook the practical advantages of writing a book.

- *Connection.* This is the one thing that all of your clients are unanimously looking for, and as coaches, it is likely one of the reasons we got into this line of work. A book establishes an instant rapport with potential clients. It shows them your world and process better than any webinar or social media post ever could. Your content will sit with them for hours, days, and weeks instead of seconds.
- *Credibility.* When you think of someone being introduced on a stage, blog, or podcast, if they wrote a book, it usually goes something like this: "I would like to introduce Joan, author of xyz." If you have heard that, it's almost guaranteed that you assigned a high level of credibility to that person even before they started talking. That is the power of a book.
- *Sales + Books = Conversion.* It's not a complex equation, but it is a powerful one. Writing a book showcases the best of you and your program, meaning that you put your best foot forward with every potential client who reads it. It becomes very likely that the reader connects with your content, which results in more sales of your high-ticket program.

- *Confidence.* In a world where there are so many coaches offering similar programs as you, it can be quite a knock to the confidence to watch your ideal customers sign with someone else. You start to wonder if it was you, or maybe your program just wasn't good enough. A book is enough to quash those thoughts. It gives you something physical to hold and look at that is an exact replication of your abilities, strengths, and commitment. Holding something that valuable is an immediate boost to your confidence.

- *Cold to hot.* When clients stumble across our services, they enter our world as cold clients. They know nothing about us. They aren't committed in any way, shape, or form, and they have only the slightest interest in us or our programs. A book can be the exact thing that turns them from cold to hot. It can be what takes them from mild interest to thinking, *I have to work with this person.*

- *Saving time.* Have you ever had a discovery call with a client that you knew right away wasn't a good fit for your program, but you had to stick around for the entire call anyway? Those suck. It's a waste of your time and theirs. A book can cut those calls out completely. By giving potential clients a view into you and your program, you can be sure that only clients who are seriously interested and a good fit will be knocking at your door, saving you time and energy.

- *Authority.* For hundreds of years, people have been stepping onto the stage and presenting themselves as authors. By making this leap, they position themselves as someone with authority. Writing a book has this kind of power. It can transform you from someone who is knowledgeable about a topic to someone who is an undeniable expert. This is the kind of authority you want to show your clients.

- *Opportunities.* I had a potential client ask me once if writing a book would get her more speaking engagements. To that, I responded, "Absolutely!" If you are looking for more exposure in your business, then writing a book is exactly what you need to do to stand out. I'm a big fan of podcasts. When I first started out, I reached out to dozens of podcasts with no response. It wasn't until I started advertising myself as an author did I finally get some traction. Hosts look for credibility, and calling yourself an author is the perfect way to showcase just that.

- *Lasting impressions.* Unlike a webinar or social media post, which sits in front of a client for a fraction of time, sometimes less than 30 seconds, a book sits with them for days, if not weeks. If you hand someone a book, they will typically read it in segments, which means they are thinking about you and your program for much longer than a post. If they read before bed, then you are the last thing they think about that day. If they read during their lunch hour, then your programs sit with them all throughout their workday. A book has a lasting impression that no other form of introduction does.

These nine benefits also double as perfectly good reasons to write a book that will boost your business, earn you credibility and authority, and help you scale way up in this world. But there is one thing missing, and it is probably the most important one of all: You need to write a book because you *want* to.

Having the drive and desire to embark on something as complex and rewarding as writing a book takes more than 10 reasons to do it. It takes motivation, passion, and commitment. You have to want it. Without that internal drive pushing you forward, you will fall into the unfortunate group of those that never do. So, what can you do to step up from *I'd like to write a book* to *I am writing a book*?

Let's start with the most basic, yet most complex, aspect: changing your mindset. You aren't about to start something impossibly hard; you are about to go on a beautiful journey of self-discovery and growth. You aren't about to lose an hour a day to writing; you are setting aside time for yourself to heal and improve every day. You aren't going to feel burned out and exhausted by this project; you are going to unleash a new sense of power and accomplishment that you never thought possible.

FOUR PHASES OF BECOMING AN AUTHOR

For a lot of aspiring authors, the idea of writing a book doesn't extend beyond the writing part. But in reality, there are four distinct phases to this process. To publish a book, you will start with the obvious: writing. Once the writing is complete, you will move into the editing phase, which is full of highs and lows as you tweak and revise your manuscript. Marketing is technically the next phase; however, I highly recommend you start marketing while you are in the writing phase. The more you talk about your book, the better. Finally, you will publish your work and claim the coveted title of author. Each phase is equally important and comes with its own set of challenges. Here is a closer look at the details of each phase.

Writing

Often thought of as "the hard part," writing gets a bad rap, but it really couldn't be more simple. It starts with finding out exactly who your reader is. This is called an *ideal reader avatar*. Once you understand who you are writing to, it's time to work on your message. Start with 10 (or more) key things you want your reader to walk away with. These will translate into your chapter headings.

Overwhelmed by how much time it takes to write a book? The trick is to set custom goals based on your availability and writing speed. With as little as 45 minutes a day, you could have your book written in just four weeks.

Editing

There are four key types of editing:

- *Developmental editing.* Acting as the big-picture assessment of your novel, this method works to assess any overarching storytelling issues. This type of editor will look at plot, structure, character development, point of view, pacing, scene dynamics, and narrative arc.
- *Line editing.* A review of your story from a line-by-line perspective. With the developmental editing done, this editor will look at how phrasing, word choice, and description affect the story and the reader's experience. They will look at things like syntax, repetition, tense, and dialogue. They will also identify sections that are overwritten and could be cut down.
- *Copyediting.* Similar to proofreading in the sense that it checks for grammar and spelling mistakes, copyediting also makes sure elements such as names, dates, and locations are treated consistently throughout the text. It entails basic fact-checking and flagging any passages that are confusing or need clarification.
- *Proofreading.* This final edit before publication entails checking for the basics of grammar and spelling mistakes.

Nervous that your book doesn't stack up against others? There is a tried and true way to quality-check your book. With your manuscript finished, there is a hidden layer known as the beta reader. This is a person or group of people that you send your book to for feedback. They are there to check your book for plot, pacing, and consistency. They are not professionals, but they can give you really amazing feedback as to how your book compares to others in its category. You may want to wait until after you receive feedback from your beta readers to send it to your professional editor(s).

Marketing

There are so many ways to market your book that it can become overwhelming—social media, blogs, podcasts, newsletters, promotions, ads, etc. My biggest tip is to pick two methods and stick with them for at least six months. The key is to pick something that you actually enjoy doing. If you don't like speaking, then stay away from podcasts. If you love writing, then consider starting a blog or approaching other blogs to appear as a guest.

Whatever methods you choose, I highly recommend you have an email list. You can establish this in several ways, but one of the best is to offer a lead magnet such as a quiz or free chapter. You need something that will solve a problem for your ideal reader so that they are willing to exchange their email for your content. Use this list to communicate directly to your readers any activity you have around your book, such as updates, behind-the-scenes information, and marketing activities you have going on.

However you choose to market your book, know that it doesn't have to be draining. Marketing can be fun if you know who you're talking to and enjoy your way of connecting with them.

Publishing

There are three types of publishing:

- *Traditional.* A publisher buys the rights to your book and publishes on your behalf. This type of publishing typically requires a literary agent that you acquire through query letters. This process can take months or years and can be full of rejection letters. It is not an easy path and requires you to be strong-hearted and tenacious.
- *Hybrid.* You hire a company to help you with various components. They might help you acquire editors, designers, and publishing platforms. This is typically a

paid service that is provided by a professional company. Similar to self-publishing, you remain the owner of your book and all its by-products, but you have someone to guide you through the nitty-gritty phases. This is a wonderful option if you are looking to publish quickly but without the headache of learning to do it all yourself.

- *Self.* You are in control and responsible for every step of the journey. Again, this is not for the faint of heart, as you take on the role of publisher. There is a lot of research and learning that goes into this path, and you might find yourself feeling rather burned out after the whole thing is said and done. It is worth it, though, so don't lose hope when things get rough.

Choosing a publishing path really comes down to what you need and desire from the process. If you are open to waiting for the right publisher to come along and guide you, then traditional publishing might be the path for you. On the other hand, if you are looking for control and speed, then hybrid or self-publishing might be the answer.

CONCLUSION

If you have made it this far, then you are already so close to joining the elite few who become published authors. Now it comes down to taking the plunge into the world of authorship. When I made the leap, I didn't let the idea overwhelm me, but rather let the process sweep me away.

Writing a book is beautiful. As with anything, there will be highs and lows, and while the end product is worth it, the journey you are about to go on is undeniably life-altering.

So, I will leave you with this: If not now, when?

ABOUT THE AUTHOR

Larissa Soehn is a well-established author and CEO of Next Page Wellness Coaching. She has extensive experience in writing, publishing, and marketing books from various genres.

As the company's founder, Larissa serves female entrepreneurs in client-based industries, namely coaches and service providers. Her mission is to help powerful women boost their business with a book. Larissa guarantees a high level of service in all aspects of writing and publishing. Her programs include one-on-one writing, editing, publishing, and marketing support for all her authors. She believes in the power of publishing a book, as she has seen firsthand what it can do for an individual and a business. Working with Larissa means gaining access to instant credibility, becoming known as an industry expert, and unlocking access to coveted speaking and networking opportunities, such as podcasts or seminars.

Larissa finds inspiration for her cause in the power of writing. She understands the excitement of finding and connecting with the ideal client. She knows the struggle and pleasures of growing a business. For Larissa, writing a book was the game-changing step that she needed to leap out of the box and move above the crowd. She became a respected and credible subject matter expert with whom her ideal clients were eagerly waiting to collaborate.

Larissa is a certified professional coach from the International Coach Academy with training in applied psychology and communications. She has developed skills that directly support the writing and promotion of exceptional books. She has knowledge of human motivation, drive, and communication methods that coincides directly with what it takes to write, publish, and market a book.

Larissa finds motivation in her family and works hard to be the best mom and wife she can be to her young daughter and wonderful husband.

Connect with Larissa:
- ➤ LarissaSoehn.coach
- ➤ NextPagePublishing@outlook.com

Chapter 3

Your Book Is a Business

by James Woosley

Be so good they can't ignore you.

—Steve Martin

Breathe in Steve Martin's words. To me, they are a challenge. I must be good. To be good, I must commit to practicing my craft. I'm obliged to study. I will most certainly sweat. But if I do those things—if I get that good—I won't be ignored. I will have confidence and boldness. I will conquer myself and my audience. I will be noticed.

As I see it, there are two things that matter when writing a book. One may allow you to succeed, but do both and you enter the arena where they can't ignore you.

The first is content. Your content is your message and your impact. It's the journey you take your readers on and the destination that satisfies them as they turn the last page. It doesn't matter if it's fiction or non-fiction. The content is the weight of your ideas and stories.

The second is the presentation. It's everything that showcases the content. It's what pushes it out into the world and into the mind of your audience. The presentation covers everything related to the medium you use—the paper and the trim size, the font size and selection, the cover and the margins. It can be the digital delivery within an ebook, flowing and changing between devices and user preferences. It can be the voice and pace and style of an audiobook. It's everything, and it all matters.

You should aim for amazing content wrapped in a beautiful presentation. An appearance that matches the quality of the content and accentuates and enhances the experience. When you do this, you have turned pro. You have committed to quality in both content and presentation and sent your book into the world to make a difference.

Quality matters. Professionalism matters.

But don't let perfection keep you from sharing your message. We can go too far with quality. Perfectionism can sharpen your sword, but it can get you stuck.

MY STORY
I am a writer. I've always wanted to write books and become an author.

I wrote my first book in the third grade. It was a fill-in-the-blank writing assignment. I illustrated it, made a cover with cardstock, and stapled the pages together. I was so proud, and I still have it.

In high school, I loved being the newspaper editor, but when I earned an ROTC scholarship, the Air Force got to decide my major. English and journalism weren't options, so I ended up in Computer Science. After all, I liked using the Mac to design the paper, right?

Computer Science was more math than words, and my creative outlets diminished over time. I graduated, joined the Air Force, and the world of words shifted into reports and performance reviews.

It would take almost 20 years for me to tap back into my core as a writer.

It started when I got the entrepreneurial bug. I joined masterminds and attended seminars. I tried teaching and coaching. I soon found a talent for strategic planning and decided to write a book on the topic.

Three years later, the book was done (with lots of procrastination and self-doubt along the way). I had no publisher. I had no audience. But I had a good book and I needed to share it with the world, so I decided to self-publish.

Then perfectionism set in. I committed to making it look and feel as real as anything from a New York City publisher. Quality matters, right? The content was good. The design had to match.

After six months of studying print-on-demand processes (and working with an editor and book cover designer), I completed the layout, submitted it to Amazon, and launched the book.

I had to prove to myself that I was good enough; that I could teach, coach, speak, and write. It was the monkey on my back.

The funny thing is that all the work to get the book published turned out to be a lot of fun. I fell back in love with page layout and design. I discovered I am more than just a writer: I am also a designer and publisher.

A few years later, a friend asked me to help her daughter publish a book of poetry. Then another friend asked for help. Soon, I was getting multiple clients and working on dozens of books. Something cool was happening.

MAKING A REAL BOOK

What makes a *real* book?

Word count? *It can't be a* real *book unless it's 100,000 words.*

Not true.

There are good books that are short and good books that are long. There are bad books that are short and bad books that are long. Your book needs to be as long as it needs to be.

Don't listen to someone who says it must be a certain number of words. There may be expectations for certain genres or audiences, but that doesn't determine if it's a real book or not.

What about your topic? *Only certain topics make for* real *books.*

False!

There are a bunch of weirdos on the internet. Find your weirdos, write a book for them, and they will read it.

Whatever your topic, there's an audience for it. Some are bigger than others, but there's somebody out there who wants your book, wants your content, and wants to hear what you have to say.

Even if it's *wEirD.*

What about sales? *It can't be a* real *book if it doesn't make the best-seller list.*

Nope!

It can be a real book even if the only copy you sell is to your mom.

Sales are not always indicative of quality. Sales are driven by marketing and promotion. You can write a powerful book that only sells a few copies. And you can write a bad book that sells millions.

"Bestseller" doesn't mean best written or most impactful.

Write for your audience, for your people, and make an impact on them. Don't worry about the sales while writing.

Just as Pinocchio wanted to become a real boy, you can write a real book. Pour your heart and soul into it and make it the best that you can possibly make it.

THE PEDESTAL

People are impressed when they find out you're an author. You have accomplished something, and they are in awe—likely because they dream of writing a book but haven't tried.

But they haven't seen the cover. They don't know the title or what it's about. And they certainly haven't read it.

But there you are.

Up on the pedestal.

The problem is, if you do a poor job and make a crappy book, they'll knock you off the pedestal.

If the writing is bad, the cover is ugly, the fonts are too big or too small, or the margins are wonky… in their mind, you're lazy, undisciplined, a phony, a fraud, whatever.

You are now *less than*. They built you up and you're worse off than you were before.

I'm not saying that you're better than they are. That's not true. But they will put you up on a pedestal and you want to honor that.

That comes down to three letters: I-T-Y.

Three letters that take you from author to *author-ity*.

You are an authority because you wrote a book. Whether you feel like you are or not, that's how they will see you. In their eyes, you are. In the marketplace, you are.

So, what does I-T-Y stand for?

It's simple: I Trust You.

Author, I trust you with my money. I trust you with my time, because it will take hours to read or listen to your book. I'm invested in you and the hope that you will teach me something or entertain me. I trust that you are worth it.

THE INTRODUCTION OF QUALITY

In the 1990s, the sitcom *Seinfeld* was at the top of the ratings. In one episode, the characters visit a friend with a new baby. They hover over the crib and see the little human staring up at them. But they don't smile. They cringe.

It was an ugly baby. And no matter what, you don't tell your friends they have an ugly baby.

They struggled to find their words until the parents were out of sight. Then all they could do was talk about the ugly baby. The same will happen with your book.

They will congratulate you. Maybe they'll share it online. But secretly, they'll say it's ugly.

We all judge books by their cover. Fair or unfair, it's the truth. Walk through a bookstore, browsing the shelves. What books get your attention? Which ones do you pick up?

If you want another perspective, visit lousybookcovers.com. Cringe and laugh all you want. Then make sure your book doesn't land there!

We know bad when we see it. But it's harder when it's your baby. Your baby looks great—even if the rest of the world thinks it's ugly.

GETTING STARTED

It's helpful to ask three questions when you are getting ready to write your book:

1. Why do you want to write a book?
This is your internal purpose. Is it about sharing your expertise? Is it to get a monkey off your back? Your purpose may be selfish, but it's okay. This is your inner motivation.

2. What results do you want from your book?
This is your external purpose. It can be about sales, but what else? What about the impact on your readers? How does it change the world?

3. What is the market for your book?
Can you expect big sales or is it a niche category that will start a movement or grow your business? Who are your readers? How will you reach them?

These are your Heart, your Hope, and your Audience. If you can answer these questions, you have what it takes to write a good book.

HOW TO CREATE A BOOK
Start Writing

My ideal writing environment is sitting in first class (using points) on a cross-country flight with my MacBook, music in my headphones, and no wifi. That's where I focus best, and I can pump out thousands of words an hour. It's a rare occurrence. But I have looked on eBay for first-class seats to build a writing cocoon. I haven't... *yet*.

When people ask me the best way to write a book, my answer isn't about a specific tool or location. It's simple: Do what works for you.

When I sit down to write, I like to start with an outline. Sometimes I listen to classes I've taught or speeches I've given. I rarely start from scratch. Do whatever has worked for you before.

Most people use a computer and programs like MS Word, Google Docs, or Scrivener. Some record themselves or use speech-to-text tools, but you can use pencil and paper.

And if the best way for you to get the words out is a hammer and chisel, tap into your inner-Fred Flintstone and get to work!

A book is a carrier of content. It is one of my favorite mediums. Maybe your content is in another format and needs to be transformed into a book. If you have a class or workshop, a keynote address, or a webinar, repurpose and reuse your content to make the process easier.

After Writing

If you're going to develop your content, you're going to have to edit it.

You should self-edit, but know that we are blind to our own mistakes. You cannot fully edit your own content. It's too close and too personal. And your brain will fill in missing words or letters because it knows they are supposed to be there.

If your friend is an English teacher, they may be able to help you go beyond a self-edit. Unless they are a professional editor, you're still going to need one.

A professional editor goes beyond fixing typos and punctuation. They will polish your work and help it flow. A great editor will make you look like a great writer.

If you are self-publishing and have a limited budget, spend it on editing over design. You can have a generic cover and layout (generic, not ugly). But you can't keep the respect of your reader if the book is too hard to read or filled with errors or typos—even if it's beautiful. Errors make it hard for the reader to care, because it's clear that you didn't think enough of them to do it properly.

Readers will forgive a few typos, but not a lot.

Design That Enhances the Content

Once the book is written and edited, it's time to make it both pretty and functional.

I'll share two design metaphors that sum up my philosophy: the CIA and the movies.

The CIA is charged with protecting the United States in a variety of ways. They stop attacks every day without anyone knowing about it. In this way, they are invisible. Good design is the same. A reader doesn't notice how the margins frame the content, making it easy to read and understand. They don't notice the font selection, sizing, spacing, or the million other details designers fret over.

Unless it's bad. Then they notice. Just like if the CIA fails to stop an attack. Then the nation wonders how on earth they could have missed it. Good design is often invisible.

Good design is also like going to the movies. I love to experience movies in a theater. After a few minutes, I forget I'm there because I'm *in* the movie, not the theater.

Until a baby cries. Or a cell phone rings. Or someone walks past me to get more popcorn. Ugh!

Now I'm back in the theater—annoyed and frustrated. Just like your readers will be if the layout is ugly or confusing. They want to lose themselves in your book. Good design lets them.

GETTING TO SALES AND PROFIT

Unless writing is the only thing you care about, you're going to have to put some energy into selling and promoting your book. Profit is a respectable goal.

But profit may not come from sales alone. Your book is a part of your business, but it's rare that the book by itself is the business.

Authors like Stephen King and J.K. Rowling only make a portion of their income from book sales. They also have movie deals and merchandise. They can command massive speaking fees.

Yes, they are authors, but they are also business owners. You need to own the business beyond your book.

In the nonfiction world, this may include speaking, training, workshops, events, masterminds, coaching, and so much more.

In the fiction world, this can include movie and television deals, speaking, training, artwork, merchandise, and more.

Look at your book as an investment. You will spend a lot of time writing it. You will spend time working with agents and pitching your book to publishers. If you self-publish, you'll spend time and money getting it printed. Either way, you'll spend time launching and promoting the book (even if you're traditionally published).

Hopefully, you can recoup that investment through book sales, but that may take some time. The bigger your platform, the bigger your audience, the more you speak, the more people you see—the faster that can happen.

But it doesn't mean it was a bad investment if it takes more than sales to make a profit on your book. Your book is a business. Don't rely on sales alone.

THE PUBLISHING SPECTRUM

There are many players in the publishing world, from the traditional publishers and small houses, to the self-publishers and vanity publishers. There are good books and bad books everywhere on the spectrum.

There are pros and cons at each point of the spectrum, except for vanity publishers. Vanity presses will take your money, won't care about your book, pump it out, and keep most of the rights and royalties for themselves. You lose control of your content and your revenue. If they go out of business, you can't even get copies of your book anymore. Stay away from vanity publishers!

My business is built around the concept of assisted self-publishing. My clients are generally self-publishing their books, but I'm doing the work for them.

I'm like a general contractor building a custom home. They don't have to worry about the plumbers and electricians and carpenters. I do the heavy lifting and give them a beautiful book that they own and control. They have the rights and royalties, not me.

I make it easy for them to have a professionally published book without having to learn the processes, tools, or design fundamentals.

My business is an accident. It started with publishing my first book. Then a friend asked for help. Then another and another. Then referrals and more referrals.

I've worked on more than 200 books. Paperback, hardcover, ebooks, audiobooks—all types of genres in both fiction and nonfiction.

Working nights and weekends, this little business was what kept food on the table and medical bills paid. At times, I was clawing through the dirt to keep it going. And while it started accidentally, what wasn't an accident is what I was doing while clawing in the dirt.

I was planting seeds. I learned that I might plant a hundred seeds before finding one that grows. I learned perseverance. I'm eating what grows and learning how to grow more.

I love books. I love publishing. It reconnected me to my past as a high school newspaper editor. The design. The words. The product. The impact.

I love the business. I love earning my own way. I love betting on myself.

I love seeing people hold their book for the first time. I love helping them share their stories with the world.

And in some small way, I get to be a part of hundreds of stories that impact thousands of people every day.

Go write your book. Someone out there is counting on it to change their life.

ABOUT THE AUTHOR

James Woosley is an underachiever—only because he's constantly expanding his potential by doing something amazing, then immediately striving for more, knowing that his mind, body, and spirit have been stretched to a new level of possibility.

A former US Air Force officer, James is the author of *Conquer the Entrepreneur's Kryptonite: Simple Strategic Planning for You and Your Business* and *Challenge Accepted!: A Simple Strategy for Living Life on Purpose.*

As a book designer and publisher, James has worked on more than 200 books, including *New York Times* bestselling author Dan Miller's self-described magnum opus, *An Understanding Heart*.

Beyond serving his clients, James is a founding member of the Satsuma City School System and former president of the Alabama Association of School Boards. James is a dedicated husband to his high school sweetheart, Heather, father to Anna and Ian, and grandfather of the most beautiful baby girl in the world, Finley.

Connect with James:
- ➤ Website: FreeAgentPress.com
- ➤ Email: james@freeagentpress.com
- ➤ Mastermind: FreeAgentPress.com/mastermind

Chapter 4

Authentically and Courageously Change Your Life by Sharing Your Story

by Dr. Kristina Tickler Welsome

You may ask, "Who am I to tell a story?"

Who are you *not* to? And what are you waiting for?

Your story matters. *You* matter. In less than 99 years, every single life you have personally touched will be over and your story will live no longer. I want to ensure that your one precious life leaves an imprint the size of your heart on this planet. I want to help you share your story with the world.

YOU ARE THE AUTHOR OF YOUR OWN LIFE

You are the author. Only you hold the pen. You are the main character, a unique one with a past chock-full of life experiences and lessons learned. Hopefully, you've made meaning out of these instances and transformed the things life has done *for* you (not *to* you) into enlightenment opportunities which generated wisdom that you now can share with others.

What are the stories you tell yourself in your own mind about where you've been and what you've gone through? You have the power to change this narrative and rewrite the story of your life. As the protagonist, you can make yourself a victim or a hero(ine). You can change the plot, switch locations, remove villains, or add a supporting cast of characters. Whenever you're ready, you can turn the page, start a new chapter, add another volume, or rewrite the whole damn book.

What are you being called to share? Is it your life story (memoir) or a life lesson? Is it your expertise or experience? Do you have something to offer which would help others traveling along the same path find hope, inspiration, or motivation? Do you want to share your deepest fantasies or your dream for a better future? Do you write simply to connect with yourself and get to know yourself better? Could this possibly serve others or the world? My guess would be that it most definitely would.

COME OUT OF THE SHADOW, YOU ARTIST!

Are you a voracious and avid reader or consumer of stories, be they from your best friend, your children, or your co-workers? Whether in a book or magazine, on TV, or your social media feed? In her book, *The Artist's Way*, Julia Cameron uses the term "shadow artist" to describe creatives who deprive themselves of their own creativity by being focused on consuming the work of others instead of creating their own. The famed psychologist Carl Jung uses the term "shadow" to describe the aspects of our own Self that we don't acknowledge or embrace fully.

Many of us suppress our desire to write and limit the attainment of this life goal by talking ourselves out of it: *I'm not really a writer... I don't have anything new to say... I don't have time due to work and family responsibilities.* Please, just stop. We make time for that which we deem to be a priority. We can't have it all... but we can have what it is we truly desire. Your dream of becoming a writer deserves to be recognized and supported with the necessary time, energy, and financial resources. Remember that this investment in yourself is also an investment in your loved ones, your career, and the world at large. Are you standing in the wings waiting to take center stage? It's time for you to stop consuming and start creating your story.

WHAT IS YOUR STORY TO TELL?

I love this question that was posed to me by one of my mentors. I use it to focus my jumbled thoughts and emotions and gain clarity. What story are you feeling called to share? Do you write daily journal entries to help you decipher the thoughts, emotions, and experiences you're working through in your life? In order to resolve ambiguity so you can make the next best step, do you write in your journal or the Notes app on your phone? Do you verbally share with others to make sense of things in order to determine how to communicate more clearly to your partner, family, friends, or colleagues? Do you enjoy sharing your thoughts with posts or reels on social media? Are you creating content for a blog, vlog, or podcast?

What is it that your soul is being called to say and put into the universe? What message is trying to come through you? Do you want to write down your whole life story, maybe just to print and leave for your children one day upon your death so they can know about the life and times of their mother, father, grandmother, or grandfather who loved them? Perhaps your story needs to be shared with the world to help others recognize they're not alone.

Your life experiences can offer hope or inspiration to others going through similar situations. If you enjoy interaction and collaboration, you may want to participate in a multiauthor book experience where a community is built around a topic of interest. You get to know like-minded individuals and work in partnership on a certain topic where you're only responsible for your own chapter or content area. You can even create a writing opportunity and cultivate your own community to write on a specific topic.

Are you ready to write a mini-book to serve as a calling card for your business and act as a warm lead to nurture potential clients so they know who you are, what you stand for, and what you're all about? This can make them aware of your services and let them know where to find you. Are you ready to write a full-length book? Did you already write it but have been afraid to share it? Whether it's personal development, a nonfiction how-to book, a novel, or your deepest fantasies, I can promise you there is a reader out there dying to settle into a comfy seat with their favorite snack or beverage in hand and dive in to read it!

WHERE DO YOU WANT YOUR STORY TO BE TOLD?

Where do you want to see your words? Privately in your journal, printed digitally, or in the pages of a print magazine or book? Just for your family or for a larger population? Do you want to see your knowledge and expertise featured in media outlets, whether as a single quote, a couple lines, or an entire article on a topic? Do you write in social media forums or for academia?

Do you want to see your name on the front cover of a book? Or do you prefer to use a pseudonym or pen name to stay anonymous so you can give your true, open, authentic, honest thoughts without fear or worry of having any impact on others? You may have an amazing story to tell, but don't want to do the actual writing work. That is when you are ready for a ghostwriter, somebody who can create a safe, supportive, nonjudgmental environment for you to verbally put your words out into the universe for them to capture and craft into the written book you want to see created.

WHY ARE YOU BEING CALLED TO SHARE THIS STORY?

In *Big Magic*, author Elizabeth Gilbert shares her insights into the mysterious magic of inspiration. I love how she describes ideas as floating all around us until they land, becoming reality only when one person accepts the calling and brings them to life. She writes, "Ideas are driven by a single impulse: to be made manifest." It is through you, the human partner, that an idea gets birthed and becomes real. Choose to become a willing partner, and the idea will come to you. Receive it with the universal support it brings, and enter into the pleasurable process of creation.

Why is sharing your story important to you? Why is its message important for others to hear? Why should it be written? When do you want it to come to fruition? My thought is that if you're reading this book, the time is *now*. You're ready to answer the call and explore what your desire to write actually looks like. This is where I love to start with my clients—envisioning how it will look and feel for this publication to come to life. From there, we determine the strategy of making the dream of becoming a published writer a reality.

We think our story is not important, that no one will care, that we couldn't possibly bear to drag our shame out of the darkness and share it with the public. But when we do, not only does it have the power to heal us, it can also go on to be the medicine that others need as well. Don't be afraid to be open and vulnerable; you just might change—or save—a life.

When I started my writing journey, I had to let go of the person I was, the stories I repeated in my mind, and the dreams I held for my future. In doing so, I got to know and love my authentic self, rewrite my narrative, start the next chapter, and envision a whole new world around and ahead of me. I chose to put pen to paper and use my journaling to make sense of my personal life that was a topsy-turvy mess, then edited and rewrote until it started to make sense to me. I realized that my life was mine to live wholeheartedly—to fail at, to learn from, to make the most of every precious moment—if only I could be brave and courageous enough to live it in my own authentic way.

Once it was written, I had to make the decision between writing a book proposal and finding an agent or figuring out how to publish myself. I had just become an international bestselling author for a chapter I wrote in a multiauthor book called *Significant Women: Leaders Reveal What Matters Most.* A dear friend of mine challenged me in the best sort of way: "Set your own metric for success, which I'm hearing you say is getting your book, *LOVE(d): The Key to Unlocking Your True Potential & Living an Authentic Life You Love,* in the hands of people you can help." So I learned how to publish and opened my own publishing house. My experience is now available to help you on your own author journey.

HOW YOU WILL FEEL WHEN YOU WRITE YOUR STORY AND CHANGE YOUR LIFE

Whether or not you choose to publish, the process of writing stories from your past can be incredibly healing and transformative. Many authors are surprised by the catharsis that comes from the simple process of putting their past on paper. I felt called to share my own lived experience and all that I learned from my own healing journey in the hope that it would help at least one person feel less alone, more hopeful, and empowered to create a life they love. I remember when I got a call from my developmental book editor, who was in tears, telling me, "You did it."

"I did what?"

"You changed one life for the better. Mine. The rest is just gravy!" I sat stunned, tears of joy filling my eyes, as I realized the impact that facing my fears with courage had. It was a pivotal moment as I realized the depth of my own potential and the power of unleashing my deepest desires and following my dreams.

I wish everyone realized they have an important story to tell. You don't have to be a professional writer or know how to make the book come to life to do it. You don't need to know how to get from idea to real-life book in hand. Just like manifesting, you don't have to know exactly how it will occur, you just need to have a desire and a belief that it can. And it will. And so it is... or something much better. It will certainly change your perspective on life. It may even lead to podcasts, speaking engagements, and business opportunities.

While journaling, meditating, reflecting, researching, failing, and learning, I discovered so much about writing and publishing, but also about giving back. Although my dream started with my own personal desire to heal and change my life by rewriting the narrative of my own story, in learning to publish and help others put their stories onto paper and into the world, the dream grew to support people even beyond the book. Recognizing that I could donate the profits from book launch sales and change even more lives—as in the case of the courageous young women of Elimu Girls at the Heri Sewing College in Malindi, Kenya—made the dream even more expansive. When we dare to heal ourselves and dream big, we can have an even greater impact on the world and give others a voice and a choice as well.

IT'S TIME TO START YOUR NEXT CHAPTER AND COURAGEOUSLY SHARE YOUR AUTHENTIC STORY

Like most things in life, getting published also takes a village. Put your intention to write in writing. Dare to share your writing dreams with a trusted friend or loved one. Ask for encouragement and support, as you don't want the self-doubt and fear that pop up to derail the process. You can work with a book coach or a developmental editor to help organize your ideas and strategize your book, your content, and your information along the way. Participating in a writers workshop or finding a writing partner with whom you can brainstorm ideas, swap drafts, and offer support and encouragement can be very helpful. Being a valued member of such a community can provide motivation, accountability, and a writing family who will join in celebrating your success.

While you may do the bulk of your writing on your own, you will still want to share your work once it's completed to get feedback. Soliciting constructive feedback and validation from friends and peers in a beta launch helps increase both excitement and confidence in your final product. No matter how good a writer you are, you'll definitely need somebody with skill to copyedit and proofread your work. Your work will need to be formatted and published. Graphic design will also need to be done, as good cover art is important. Marketing images and promotional materials, as well as a pre-launch campaign, will help ensure a successful book launch, five-star reviews, and continued book sales.

UNLOCK THE TRUEST VERSION OF YOURSELF

Are you ready to rewrite your own authentic story and live a life you love? You can get started by answering the call to write. The key to this story lies within you, in your pocket. It's up to you to use it to unlock your full potential and share your story with the world. I wish to encourage you to pick up the pen and put the very first word on the page. The possibilities are endless and the potential exists within each one of you.

Once you've made the decision to write your story and change your life, the next step is to explore your story and determine your focus. It's time to mine your life for the moments (both large and small) that have made you who you are. You will likely be surprised at what you discover about yourself.

I found it imperative for myself as an author to get to know, like, and trust myself before I could successfully write to connect with a reader. So often we tend to focus on the story itself and how to tell it in a way that draws in the reader. I discovered that once I connected with myself to identify and focus my own unique lens as the storyteller, it became clear why the story needed to be told. I was then able to bring the human connection and healing element necessary for all good stories.

Meet yourself where you are. Take the time to rediscover just who it is you are and what you are being called forth to say. Tune in to the deep wisdom and guidance of your heart, mind, body, and soul. And trust that the Universe will provide the information, knowledge, inspiration, motivation, accountability, and skills needed to empower you to reach your full potential on this path of self-exploration and ultimate success.

ABOUT THE AUTHOR

Dr. Kristina Tickler Welsome is a doctor of physical therapy, owner of The Key to Wellness and The Key Publishing, a self-love and life-desire coach, and an international bestselling author and publisher. Her decades of professional experience with patients, students, and clients make her coaching effective, efficient, and easily integrated into your life. Her passion is to support the well-being and healing of your heart, mind, body, and soul as you learn to love your authentic self. Tina will empower you to become the author of your own life story as you discover unconsidered possibilities, remove barriers to success, and unlock your full potential to live a creative life that you love. Her life journey prepared her to use her voice to amplify the voices of others and create even more impact in the world. You can find her living her best life as a mom of three divine masculine men-in-the-making and expanding her own highest potential as a perfectly imperfect human being.

Connect with Kristina:
- ➤ Website: thekeytowellness.net
- ➤ Facebook page: facebook.com/kristina.welsome
- ➤ Facebook group: facebook.com/thekeytowellness.net
- ➤ Twitter: @DrTinaWelsome
- ➤ Instagram: @thekeypublishinghouse and @thekeytowellness.tina
- ➤ LinkedIn: linkedin.com/in/drkristinawelsome
- ➤ Email: tina@thekeytowellness.net

Chapter 5

The Book Mumma

by Brigid Holder

Through writing, we are creatively releasing past trauma, and in doing so, we allow others permission to do the same.

—Brigid Holder

COMING HOME

I never expected to be the 'Book Mumma' or to love it as much as I do. As a young woman, I didn't know what I wanted to do and never dreamed of someday becoming a writer. Life unfolded, and I found myself moving further and further away from feeling fulfilled at work, as a mother, or in any social setting.

I travelled a lot when I was in my early twenties, as I found it soul-enriching. Heartbreak stopped the travel for some time and I fell in love again, got married, and had children. My search for what lit me up drifted off for a long while. Instead, I did what all good girls did: worked in various administrative jobs and became general manager and second-in-charge at large organisations, managing millions in budgets but never quite feeling fulfilled. I had to grow into my roles and study topics that I found boring and mundane. Managing people was probably the only part I truly enjoyed. Then, in my late forties, something unexpected happened.

I had been working with a business coach for months. She told me that many of her clients spoke of one day wanting to write a book and enquired if I, too, had this desire. I didn't. But if she was doing it, I was in! Monique Alvarez introduced me to the world of publishing with our first book, where it all began for me, aptly titled *Trailblazers*.

Intrigued by the idea of helping women bring their stories to life and being a part of the literary world, I wanted to jump in. Instead, I dipped my toe in. When I completed the publishing certification course through Monique's AMA Publishing, I felt like I was slower out of the blocks than the other women. I felt I was holding myself back. Little did I know, I was on the precipice of finding my all-time high in life, which would repeat over and over every time I contributed to or published a book.

Wanting more, I created The Art of Grace Publishing House, a tribute to my grandparents, Art and Grace, who were both shining loves and lights in my life. Here I get to play in the arena that sets my heart on a path of expansion every day.

Diving into my publishing journey, I found the stories of others fascinating. Reading manuscripts, working with women who were aspiring or published authors, and witnessing and holding space for them as they took their own emotional rollercoaster rides was a privilege.

Ultimately, seeing their books brought to life quite simply made my heart expand! I felt like I'd come home.

BECOMING THE 'BOOK MUMMA'

As I gained more experience in publishing, I began to develop a reputation I am grateful for and so very proud of. I am known for my balance in allowing authors to stay in flow, paying careful attention to not get stuck in detail; my ability to connect with women of all walks of life; and my unwavering dedication to making every book I am invited to collaborate on the best it can be.

Soon enough, the authors started calling me the 'Book Mumma'. I care about their work and their story, and I am always there to offer support and guidance along the way. At first, I didn't like it, but now I love the nickname. In the beginning, I attached the term 'book mumma' to my old self who did not love motherhood, did not find it fulfilling, and did not feel at ease as a mum. As it stuck, I searched deep within and spoke to seven authors who used the term frequently. Now, it represents everything I want to be—someone who nurtures and cares for the books and the female authors I work with. It's a title I now wear with great pride.

> *Brigid, aka 'the Book Mumma', dances the perfect balance between nurturing advisor and confidant, whilst being a powerful and wise businesswoman. She guides, supports, and understands all the highs and lows of the writing process, but then kicks it up a gear to lead you and your book to succeed in the publishing and launching stage and beyond.*
>
> —Kelly Paardekooper,
> Pharmacist, Intuitive Guide, Author

HITTING THE INTERNATIONAL BESTSELLER LIST

My reputation grew, my energy catapulted to the next level, and I began to work with women who were on their own mission. To be of service in this way and feel the joy expressed through these women allows me to expand even more. Working from this heart-centred place, I am easily hitting goals for them and our publishing house.

The books published by our team at The Art of Grace Publishing House make an impact. They have the capacity to alter the lives of those who read them as well as the women writing them. Our aim is to publish books that allow women to see what is possible, and it continues to fill me with so much awe and gratitude.

Our books, and those that I contribute to, often quickly become best-sellers in the author's home country and are soon picked up around the world. Witnessing a book climb the charts is a mix of excitement and disbelief. I had never imagined that something I helped create could become so successful. But I know that it is a testament to the work the authors put into the book. The work is not just writing; it involves the emotions of the authors and the consideration to others the books may impact as well. The journey from writing to publishing is like a trauma rehab in a small, contained timeframe. As the Book Mumma, I am there to hold the authors' hand and guide them—not force, not push, but guide. I consider it an honour that they allow me so deep into their vulnerability.

The success of that first book stays with me as we work on new projects. I love working with authors to bring their stories to life and leave their legacy in the world. Each book, like each woman, is unique. But the books all share a common thread: they are the best they can be and bring a new perspective to the world to enable change.

I continue to work with authors from all walks of life, helping them to write their stories, and launching their legacies into the world. I cherish the relationships publishing has allowed me to build. I am extremely proud to be known as the Book Mumma, the woman who allows authors time and space whilst supporting them to birth their stories.

The success of each book is a source of pride for the entire team at The Art of Grace Publishing House, but more than anything, I love the process of creating something meaningful with each author I work with. For me, it's about more than just selling books. It's about connecting with people and helping them to share their message with the world.

FINDING PASSION

Looking back on my journey, I'm struck by how unexpected it all was. I had never planned to become a writer, an author, or a publisher, and I certainly never expected to hit international bestseller lists. Despite the unexpected twists and turns, I know that this is exactly what I am meant to be doing. In all these stories, mine and those of others in the books we publish, I found my passion, my calling, and I wouldn't have it any other way.

I know that there are plenty of challenges in the world of publishing. It's a tough industry, and success is never guaranteed. But I believe that if you work hard and care deeply, you can make a difference. Your story matters, you deserve to be a bestseller, and the world deserves to hear from you!

And for me, that's what it's all about, making a difference. For each book I publish and each author I work with, I know that I am helping to create something meaningful. That, to me, is the ultimate reward.

May the ripple effect that the publishing of stories creates continue to make an impact in the lives of women and men around the world, and may I have the privilege to continue to be involved in this work for many years to come.

ABOUT THE AUTHOR

Brigid Holder of The Art of Grace Publishing House pushes the boundaries of publishing. Her literary prose spotlights empowerment, truth-telling, and women breaking barriers. Believing stories have the power to impact and shift multigenerational patterns, her goal is to collaborate whilst leaving a legacy that evokes heartfelt wisdom and honours heroines cultivating a blazing literary trail for emerging authors. When not writing, publishing, or being the Book Mumma—and a *USA Today* bestselling author—she can be found hiking with her boys, fostering her own empowerment, and watching her family create lasting memories surely to later be found bound in a curated collection of words.

Connect with B:

➤ brigidholder@gmail.com
➤ facebook.com/brigid.holder

Chapter 6

My Relationship with Writing as Release

by K LaFleur-Anders

Writing has always been my first love. It has been good to me and for me. Our relationship includes even exchanges of energy, care, and healing. When we are together, we vibe. No matter how I'm feeling, writing allows me to express myself without judgment. It sees me and ushers me into a place to be heard and seen. Writing embraces and accepts me for who I am and permits me to just be.

Up until my late twenties, I wrote down everything. In my journals I shared what I did each day, who I encountered, what we discussed, what I ate, etc. If it happened, I wrote it down. I also wrote poetry, because with poetry there are no rules. It didn't have to rhyme, and honestly, it didn't even have to make sense to anyone else but me. I never went back to read the poetry I wrote or what happened days before. I wrote, released, and moved on. My writing was expressive, therefore my journals were filled with lessons I could one day reflect on, but I never did. I didn't revisit journal entries to remember or reflect, I just needed somewhere to release what I was feeling and thinking.

When I got married, I stopped writing. Almost immediately, we had my first son, moved to Texas, and started a new life in a new place where we knew not one person. Life had completely changed and suddenly I was living every moment of it without a release. I tried different outlets like working out, volunteering, and focusing on a corporate career, but none of those things gave me what writing gave to me. I loved my role as a wife and mom at home, and my family will always mean the world to me. I loved my job and giving back to my community. But something was missing. Writing was missing.

When I realized how long it had been since I journaled, I immediately understood why I had been overwhelmed and depressed at times. It was because I forgot about my first love. I forgot about our relationship and how it had been there for me. I had to get back to it, but I had no idea how. I had gotten busy with tons of new commitments and I didn't see where I could fit writing in again. I was trying to find a space for it. It was challenging, and at some point, I just gave up.

Years went by before I decided to give my relationship with writing another try. How did we reunite? I was browsing through Facebook one day and a post caught my eye. I stared at it for a few seconds and suddenly felt this boost of courage. I wanted to test the chemistry between writing and myself to see if we still had a vibe. So I applied to be a contributing writer for a popular mom's blog. I was shooting my shot. Even though I had convinced myself that I wouldn't be disappointed if I wasn't chosen, I was lying to myself. I knew I would be. I wanted to be chosen. I needed to be chosen. I needed writing, and for the first time, I felt it needed me too. I had acquired more life experiences and matured tremendously—I had tons to share with other people. I wanted to inspire, encourage, and share the message of self-grace.

However, I also knew that if I were chosen, my relationship with writing would become public. Many people know about my love for it, but no one had ever read it. Writing would not just be for me anymore. A blog that reached thousands was much different than a journal that was just for me. I knew that if I were chosen, I wouldn't just *do* the act of writing; I would *be* a writer.

RETURNING TO MY FIRST LOVE

In January 2020, I received an email that set my heart on fire. I was chosen to join the team of blog contributors and I was ecstatic, to say the least. I remember being overjoyed because I was returning to express myself in a way my soul understood. I was getting back to me. The feeling of joy and relief was intense. However, 2020 soon became a life-changing year for me in multiple ways. In addition to Covid, I started experiencing many shifts and transitions in my friendships, career, family relationships, and health. It felt as if the world stopped moving, but everything in my life picked up speed. I was confused, overwhelmed, dizzy, and looking for a way off of the rollercoaster ride I was on. Thankfully, I had writing to help me release what I was feeling, and this time I was sharing it with others who were likely feeling the same way.

Quarantine was hard but a blessing. It's where I got to pause, breathe, and write. Although my life was experiencing many shifts, those moments of expressive writing helped me and others put things into perspective. It opened up the vision I had for myself as a writer and what I wanted to write about. It was during 2020 and 2021 that I settled into what I was called to do and how I was called to do it. Writing and I had found our home in women's wellness. I became a certified wellness coach and started using expressive writing to encourage women to create, heal, and grow.

As I continued to write, I became more comfortable with expressing my thoughts and feelings publicly. I had also reintroduced intimacy back into my relationship with writing because I was journaling again. Writing helped me become more creative. I started hosting wellness workout parties for women and webinars with panel guests. We talked about rest and how to fill your cup first. We took moments to breathe and share love. After every event, I received text messages and calls from women who said they'd needed something that was said or just that hour-and-a-half to invest in themselves. Their feedback and support fueled me. It made me write even more.

Writing also helped me through my healing and growth processes. And the beautiful part of it all is that I wasn't so focused on who hurt me or anything external. I was focused on what I could do differently and how I could improve, so that's what I wrote about. Writing became a tool that helped me develop as a person while simultaneously helping me become more visible professionally. It was a beautiful sight to see, but I had no idea where it was taking me until I received yet another email.

THE JOURNEY FROM WRITER TO AUTHOR TO PUBLISHER

One of my best friends invited me to join her as a co-author in a multiauthor book. I was thrilled, but also nervous. I was being asked to expand my territory and that scared me a bit. I went from writing for myself, to not writing, to writing for women readers located in one city, to literally writing for readers across the globe. No exaggeration is happening here. The publisher of the book lives in Germany and is an international bestselling author many times over. Several of the contributors in the book were international bestselling authors too.

So, was I nervous? Umm… yes. I had found my voice and tone and was comfortable with it. But now I was being asked to pump up the volume and get even louder. I was being prompted to share my heart with more people, which meant more visibility. For a naturally private person, that can be scary. I'd like to consider myself somewhat of an extrovert, but this was over the top. However, I knew that it wasn't about me anymore. Once I was chosen to contribute to the blog, that "about me" stuff was over. Besides, our purpose never really is about us. I mean, yes, it's the purpose that *we* are walking in, but we're walking in it to be a resource and light for others.

After submitting my chapter and moving through the beautiful publishing process, I decided that I wanted to create the same experience for women writers. Becoming an international bestselling author was just the cherry on top of a combination of sweet everythings that happened to me and for me in this process. Starting my publishing company gave me yet another way to celebrate and nurture my relationship with writing. This time, I was bringing others into the fold and supporting them as they followed their dreams of becoming a published author.

I dreamt of becoming a published author when I was in my teens, but back then it was very difficult to do. If you weren't someone famous, a traditional publisher wouldn't blink in your direction. Thankfully, we don't have to worry about that anymore. Thanks to hybrid publishing, I became a published author and am now creating the same opportunities for other women with that dream.

My first book as a publisher, *Transitions,* made me a bestselling author a second time. In it, the authors expressed how we overcame and learned from challenging life transitions. This book was timely for me because I had just grown my way out of some tough ones. Almost immediately after the first book was published, we were planning the second book. It was a high I couldn't come down from, and that was true for most *Transitions* writers as well. However, this time we were taking a slightly different approach. Instead of writing about our experiences only, we were using expressive writing to write love letters to someone else. I wanted this book to be filled with letters of encouragement from one mom to another. Why? Not just because Mother's Day was drawing near and I was planning a huge event to celebrate the launch of the book and Chestnut Publishing House (even though the strategy behind that decision worked out beautifully). But mostly because I knew moms who needed encouragement, and I did too. When we plant seeds, we reap a harvest that both we and others can eat from.

PIECES TO MY PURPOSE PUZZLE

During this process, my friend Monique was struggling with her health. She was a divorced mom of four who always had her kids hooked to her hip. I often called her supermom. She loved her kids and they loved her too. Monique was the most giving person I knew, and I had no doubt that she would say yes to contributing to the book. Besides, who better to encourage a mom than a supermom? It was in her heart to give what she had to others, even to her detriment sometimes. Monique was a talented artist, and although she doubted her ability to be a "good" writer, she poured her heart into her chapter. She wrote a letter to moms but most importantly, her chapter described her love for each one of her babies.

After she submitted her chapter for *From One Mother to Another*, she told me that writing it was therapeutic for her. Being able to express what she felt in moments she never took the time to think about again helped her realize just how strong, courageous, and badass she was. It made her realize how strong, courageous, and badass all women are. She was able to release some weight she had been carrying around for years in a little over a thousand words. As her friend, I was thrilled, and it made me so happy. As a publisher, I knew that I was on the right path and walking toward my purpose.

My conversations with Monique confirmed that the space I was holding for women to create, heal, and grow through writing was spot-on. We were both excited about it because she knew whatever I was doing, there was a space for her. I was there for her just like she was there for me. Every conversation thereafter was about how we would continue to improve together. They were about the next book, getting healthier, and being our very best selves.

We lost Monique last year. Losing her felt like an earthquake at my core and unearthed many things for me. At the very beginning, I thought my ever-flowing tears would somehow be a relief. After all, crying is a release. Spending time with her children was a way for me to hug her again through them. But every time they would leave or I would hang up the phone, I would cry again. There never seemed to be enough tears to bring me relief. Then I remembered our conversation about how therapeutic expressive writing was for her. In the depths of my grief, I had forgotten that this was an opportunity for writing to show up for me again. So I leaned in, and I wrote this chapter so you can lean in too. Although Monique is no longer physically here, she's here and will always be. She left me with gifts—her children and the unquestionable fact that expressive writing is therapeutic and a great way to focus on yourself, even if only for a moment. I will love and miss her always.

FIND YOUR VOICE, TELL YOUR STORY

As an expressive storyteller, I always lead with a story. I love sharing my experiences to assure you that I'm not just sharing what I heard or have witnessed in someone else's life. I share my story to assure you that my lived experience is what fuels what I do. Now, here's where I summarize my experiences to encourage you.

If you're reading this book, you're either trying to find your voice, find your way in the publishing world, or both. You have a voice and it needs to be heard. You're in the right place. As a creative wellness coach, I can help you find it using a writing-for-wellness holistic approach through journaling. That's how I found my voice and my way. No matter what you have been through, where you are, or where you're going, you have a story to tell, and my mission is to help you tell it. Journaling sounds simple, but the work requires you to focus on who you are before focusing on what you desire to do. You will be challenged to prioritize your well-being to do or write well. It's during the process of journaling that you will be able to express how you feel in areas such as your relationships, emotions, body, and mental health, which can all either boost or suppress your creativity.

Through workshops, group coaching, speaking, my podcast, and various published works, I hope to promote mental, physical, social, and emotional well-being to help women tap into a level of creativity that will allow them to be their truest selves. Together, we peel back the layers in these safe spaces curated for creativity, healing, and growth. We unearth those weights that keep you stuck so you can plant new seeds in their place, nurture them through writing, and watch them grow.

Not all of my clients are interested in becoming published authors, but those who are have found expressive journaling to be an effective avenue to reach their goals. For writers interested in the fiction genres, we use journaling to rewrite our stories and experiences. As we express our thoughts and emotions about what we've experienced in life, we work to change the characters, settings, and even the outcome of a life-changing event to create a more favorable ending. We tell socially impactful stories that will be authentic to your voice and message and use them to educate, inform, uplift, and inspire readers. What fiction writers often leave the experience with is gratitude and a more positive outlook. Writers acknowledge their past traumas without allowing them to define who they are.

As you establish your relationship with expressive writing, you will discover the beauty of taking your time and learning how to just be as you continue to move through each day. The creative process is all about alignment and flow, and writing creates the space for you to find yours. You don't have to rush it. You can take your time and allow the process to run its course. Writing is not judgmental. You don't need professional training or to show up as anyone else. It allows you to be who you are, and it welcomes you as you are. It's in the process of expressive writing through journaling that you become a storyteller.

After all, who better to tell your story than you?

ABOUT THE AUTHOR

K LaFleur-Anders is a three-time bestselling author, founder and CEO of Chestnut Publishing House, and creative wellness coach who uses a writing-for-wellness approach to help women heal. Through speaking, published works, and her podcast, *Reset with K*, she promotes mental, physical, social, and emotional well-being for women in business.

Roots & Branches, a local Austin-area community of storytellers, was created by K to provide a nurturing space for women writers and creatives to grow. Embracing Chestnut's heart-centered formula of wellness + writing + community, R&B embodies K's belief that fruitful connections and collaborations contribute to one's creative well-being.

Named by *Austin Woman Magazine* as a "woman to watch," K has been featured on *Spectrum 1 Austin News* and in various publications, including *Voyage*. She is also a recipient of the Brainz Magazine 2022 CREA Global Awards.

K and her family live in Round Rock, Texas, where they enjoy hiking, football, and trying new foods.

Connect with K:
- ➢ LinkedIn: linkedin.com/in/k-lafleur-anders
- ➢ Instagram: instagram.com/klafanders
- ➢ Chestnut Publishing House: @chestnutreads on FB and IG

Chapter 7

Overcome Your Writing Blocks and Align with Your Inner Magick

by Ruth Fae

Stories contain magick. Words weave spells. They make us feel, think, understand, and question. They pass on knowledge, history, and warnings. Through words, we share, connect, celebrate, grieve, and inspire. We pass on traditions, culture, and experiences from generation to generation, thus keeping the essence of our experiences alive. From cave paintings to novels, songs to fairy tales, poetry to epic tomes, storytelling is part of human nature.

How many times have you read something and thought, *I needed to hear that today*? Our stories deepen our relationships and understanding of each other and ourselves. They help us heal from challenges and celebrate the wonderful moments that life sends our way. When our stories resonate, we connect. Sharing what we've learned, how we've grown and healed, helps other people do the same. Stories give us a way to understand ourselves and others, and to find our way when we're feeling lost. Sometimes it's simply helpful to know that someone else feels the same way.

Whether you're a 'writer', a 'published author', or not, telling your stories is often incredibly difficult. It can be scary, challenging, and sometimes downright impossible to get your story out of your head and heart. Uncertainty, insecurity, fear, lack of worth, or simply not being able to find the right words can cause even the most prolific writer to consider a new career. Even Stephen King talks about his battles with writer's block. For an aspiring author, this challenge can feel overwhelming and disheartening. It certainly did for me. Ultimately, this guided my journey from freelance writer, to copywriter, to copywriting coach, then the work I now adore as an intuitive writing coach and editor. You don't have to do this alone.

THE POWER AND BEAUTY OF CO-CREATION

There is immense power in co-creation. As a freelance journalist, I worked predominantly alone, although guided by my editors. When I trained as a copywriter, the expectation was to take a client brief, do the work, and hand it back, with some discussion between the first and final drafts. Although it took me a little while to recognize, this didn't feel right for me. There was an inherent detachment between 'client' and 'service provider' that simply didn't sit well. It didn't take long for me to realise that I needed to get to know my clients, feel their energy, and work together in energetic flow to create content for their businesses.

I began to work with business owners, sharing my writing and editing knowledge to co-create websites, blogs, and books for business owners.

No one knows their business, their reason why they do what they do, and what drives them better than the business owners themselves. Thankfully, the Universe stepped in and gifted me with clients who showed me the way to reconcile the disconnect I felt. I learned how to work with people in a beautiful, nonjudgmental space of shared knowledge and wisdom that then transformed into the intuitive writing coaching and editing I do today.

STEP ONE: IDENTIFY AND WORK THROUGH YOUR WRITING BLOCKS

I've always loved to write. As a child, during high school and university, in the many and varied job roles I've held over the years, I enjoyed the act of creating connection through words. But somewhere along the line, I lost my mojo. Imposter syndrome and self-doubt took a significant hold, and I stopped writing.

Then copywriting came into my life. Although starting my first business was daunting, I discovered that I was much more confident writing for other people, helping them to 'find their voice', teaching them all the tips and tricks I'd learned over the years, creating content that helped to grow their businesses, and giving them the courage to speak out about their passions. But write my own story? That was never going to happen.

Then my life turned upside down. Shattered, I had to put myself back together, so I began to do some deep inner work. In going through this transformative process, I rediscovered the voice hiding under the pain and the overwhelming expectations I placed on myself. Now, I'm writing daily—in my journal, on my laptop; I've got notebooks everywhere. Yes, I write for my work, which I love, but most importantly, I write for me. And through that, I'm healing and growing in many ways.

WRITING BLOCKS

Writing blocks get in our heads and stop us putting words onto paper. But they can be overcome if they are explored and reframed and we are open to the possibility of creative solutions.

I can't write

One of my clients has dyslexia. It's very difficult for her to get words on paper (or a screen) and she has a distinct lack of confidence in her writing ability. But this doesn't mean she can't tell her stories and connect with her people. It simply means there's something in the way of getting her thoughts out of her head.

I hate writing

Another client desperately desired to write a book, but absolutely hated the thought of sitting down 'to write'. It made her feel cross and uncomfortable, and she could not get in the right headspace. During our first coaching session, we discovered that the reason she struggled dated back to high school when an English essay she was proud of was destroyed by her teacher's red pen. That memory stayed with her, and for 25 years, she's hated writing and lacked confidence and belief in her abilities. *Can she write?* Absolutely. *Does she have amazing things to say?* Yes, she does. But the fear of the 'red pen' blocked her. Creating a safe, noncritical, and energetically supported space helped her to trust, open up, and release her words.

I don't have time

Early in my copywriting days, I worked with a financial advisor who wasn't confident that she could write, or speak well on video, because English is her second language. And when she did try, it took a long time. So I suggested that she record her thoughts. It was the perfect solution. When she had an idea for a blog post, she'd record it on her phone (often while walking her dog in the morning), send it through to me, and I'd write the content she required. She struggled with the *act* of writing, but storytelling and connecting with her clients and wider audience were important to her, so we worked together to make it happen.

Confident and skilled writers also need support

I recently had the pleasure of working with a wonderful woman who had written the first draft of her chapter for a multiauthor collaboration. She knew what she wanted to say, but when she wrote it down, she felt overwhelmed. She thought it was 'rubbish', wasn't happy with what she'd written, and felt blocked about where to go next. So we spent an hour-and-a-half together talking about the areas that could be improved or needed clarity for the reader. By the end of that session, and after I'd edited her chapter, she was happy and proud of her contribution. She felt fully confident that she could submit to the publisher knowing that she and her business were represented in the best possible way.

Do you recognize any of these blocks or feelings about writing? I invite you to take a few minutes to think about what kind of blocks you come up against.

> *How do you feel if you have to write something for personal reasons or for work?*

> *Feel into what prevents you from writing your book, chapter, or blog post.*

> *What stops you from creating a social media post that shares something meaningful with your clients?*

> *Why are you struggling to tell your story?*

See what comes up for you. When you identify your writer's blocks, you can overcome them.

WRITERS ARE BRAVE SOULS

Two other significant blocks often come up, particularly for solo book authors and contributors to collaborative book projects. And, funnily enough, they are the opposite sides of the same coin:

> *Will anyone read it?*

What if I pour my heart and soul onto this paper, tear myself inside out, risk everything, feel nervous, go through all these emotions, and no one reads it? Is there any point?

When your story is engaging, interesting, well written, easy to read, and told from your heart and soul, it will find its way to the people who need to hear your message. This is where the knowledge and skills of a writing coach and a professional editor come into play.

What if someone reads it?

What will my parents, kids, friends, or colleagues think when they read my work?

Will I be judged? What if I offend someone?

The thought of anyone reading your book can be daunting. Self-doubt kicks in. Worry takes over about what people will think if they don't agree, don't like the way you write, or don't care for what you have to say. And on the flipside comes the fear that your reader *will* like it and send it farther out into the universe. Once you publish your book, blog, or social media post, it is out of your control. Even though I've always loved to write, this 'what if' fear was a massive block that I've worked hard to heal. But in going through that experience time and again, I've learned how to help other people navigate the fears that accompany putting part of your soul out there for the world to see.

SHARE WHAT FEELS RIGHT

You don't owe your readers any more than you are prepared to give. It's how it's written that matters; you can convey emotion and hint at events without going into graphic details.

There are ways to protect you and the person or people you're writing about: changing names, details, places, or writing about the event as if it happened to someone else. There are methods to navigate sensitive issues. So, if fear about this aspect of writing holds you back, acknowledge it and address it with your coach, editor, or publisher. Industry professionals can help you work through this and find clarity, so when your book is published, you can feel fully confident.

Scary and exhilarating, writing a book is baring your soul. Authors are brave people who face their fears, delve into their depths, draw out their stories, emotions, and beliefs, then put them on display. Why do we do it? Because there is an incredible joy to be found when you surrender to the process and release your story—first to your editor and publisher, then to the world.

STEP TWO: ALIGN WITH YOUR INNER MAGICK; CONNECT WITH YOURSELF AND YOUR READER

This part of your writing journey involves defining who you are as an author and drawing your story from your head, heart, and soul. This is where you align with your magick—that beautiful spark inside you that desires to share your knowledge, wisdom, guidance, and even warnings with your readers.

During the last few years, I've gone through a significant healing process that involved rediscovering and deeply exploring my spirituality and intuition. As I learned and grew, as I filled my mind, body, and soul with knowledge of the connection we share with each other and the Universe, my business naturally transformed in synergy.

When I began to align with my inner magick, I was very clearly led into the space of co-creation that has now become my passion and driving force. I feel incredibly honored when a client trusts me with their story. And that's why I choose to use the word 'intuitive' in my process. Working with an author is exactly that—a feeling, a knowing, an understanding that we are speaking the same unspoken, intuitive language. It's divine. It's beautiful. And I love it.

As an intuitive writing coach, I guide you to tell your story. As an editor, I sprinkle magick onto your words. My focus is the in-between of 'telling' and 'publishing'. Every story must go through three distinct aspects of editing:

- Structural/Developmental
- Line/Copy
- Proofreading

In my work with authors, coaching and all three aspects of editing flow together. And as I bring in my intuition and energetic connection to the author and their story, it all comes together in a beautiful, safe, and nonjudgmental space of co-creation.

Aligning with your inner magick involves learning who you are, why you do what you do, why you want to tell your story, and who your audience will be. On top of all that, it's about finding *your* voice and clarifying the message that you want to share with the world. It's very easy to step into someone else's voice, to write in a way that you think you 'should' be heard. But that's not authentic. Identifying and using your voice, sharing your personal experiences and wisdom, is way more powerful than trying to be, or sound like, someone else.

Bring the true *you* into your story. That will connect you with the person who needs to read your words.

STEP 3: CREATE A STORY THAT PERFECTLY REPRESENTS YOU (AND YOUR BUSINESS) AND FILLS YOUR HEART WITH JOY

Writing, coaching, and editing all flow together to create the message you desire to share with the world.

Co-creation is about finding your voice and being empowered; feeling safe to be vulnerable and step into a space where you are unsure. It's about being courageous and confident to share your thoughts, first with yourself and then with your wider audience.

As I moved further into writing coaching, I began to see how my personal healing and intuitive work also supported me in guiding my authors. And I came to understand that my role, what I now view as my divine purpose in this life, is to create a safe and nonjudgmental space for writers to tell their story, to trust me with their innermost thoughts and fears. I am their writing doula, here to guide and be with them as they birth their book.

During 2020, I was blessed to edit a book written by a mother and son. As they told their individual stories and we wove them together to tell their moving, heartbreaking, yet inspiring and changemaking tale, they experienced intense healing of their relationship with themselves and each other. It was a beautiful gift and honor to hold space throughout their journey and witness their understanding and transformation unfold.

Recently, I worked with a contributor to a multiauthor book. Again, she faced blocks in the *writing* of her story, but not in the *telling* of it. She spoke for two hours, in her words and her voice. She expressed everything she needed to, and as she processed the emotions that arose through the telling of her story, she began to recognize where she desired to heal. Then she graciously handed it over to me to form a story that shares her life experiences, lessons, message, and inner magick into a chapter that connects with and helps others.

Co-creation not only helps a person tell their story, it also guides and supports them through the process of exploration and healing. As an author, to know you have someone beside you to listen, share your worries (and your tears), celebrate the breakthroughs, and help you create a magickal story that resonates with the reader who needs to hear your message is a blessing. It's trust. It's surrender. It's doing it together.

EDITING AND STORYTELLING ARE INTERTWINED

Often, people view coaching and editing as two separate jobs. They can be—I do, at times, work only as an editor—but to me, they do not exist individually. They are interwoven in the art of crafting a story that engages, connects with, and inspires the reader.

You, the author, are the storyteller. Your coach helps you draw out the story. Your editor then forms that story into something other people read and enjoy. Editing brings the reader into the story because they're also part of this experience, and we can't forget them. Yes, it is about grammar, punctuation, voice, and flow, but it also involves bringing intention, energy, and connection into the publishing journey.

Viewing this process as a whole ensures that your story engages your reader from beginning to end, expresses and conveys emotion, and creates connection in the way that both the reader and author desire. Ultimately, your book or chapter will tell a complete story that ties together beautifully in a unique bundle of you that you feel confident to share with the world.

BECOME A CONFIDENT PUBLISHED AUTHOR

As an author, your role is to find a coach, editor, and publisher you trust. Our role as industry professionals is to honor you and your story. If you burn to tell a tale, then it is worth telling. And any of the writing blocks, doubts, fears, or lack of self-worth that get in the way can be overcome—if we do it together.

A writing coach supports you as your story leaves your conscious and subconscious mind. An editor holds your words safe while sprinkling them with editing magick. Together, we create a story that is relevant, engaging, and flows beautifully. We transform it into the most visceral, sparkly, gorgeous version it can be—and it's all yours.

Co-creation through intuitive writing coaching and editing is different with every client. There is no blueprint; that's not how it works.

And it's certainly not how intuition and energy flow. As authors with individual stories to tell, you have different needs, worries, doubts, blocks, and challenges that arise, depending on what you're writing and why you've chosen to write it.

No matter how difficult it may feel or the roadblocks you may face, know you are worth being seen. You are worth being heard. Understand that not only does this process bring inner healing for you, your bravery in sharing your story will also help other people understand and navigate their experiences in life. Sharing your story with the world, and making sure it is everything it can be so that your readers can connect, resonate, learn, and grow from your words, is a sacred gift.

Storytelling is shared, beautiful, magickal, and divine.

JOURNAL PROMPTS

Journaling is an amazing way to connect with your inner thoughts and feelings. My journal musings are also super helpful references. When I feel the urge to write but don't know where to start, or I'm stuck along the way, they kick-start the process and get me moving. It's also good writing practice!

Journaling is for you. No one else reads it unless you want them to. So it doesn't matter if you use bullet points, half-finished sentences, simple words, phrases, or make the page pretty with colorful pens— this is all YOU!

Prompts to Align with Your Inner Magick

I invite you to think about what inner magick means to you.

- How do you feel aligned with this in your work, in your day-to-day life, or in your private thoughts?
- What gifts do you bring to the people around you?

Prompts to Identify Writing Blocks
- Where do you feel stuck or uncomfortable?
- What is stopping you from writing?
- Where does your fear come from? Can you think of any specific events that have caused you to feel this way?

Prompts for Crafting Your Magickal Story
- What do you want to write about?
- What stories do you want to share? Why do you want to share them?
- Who do you want to connect with? What message do you have for them?
- What do you want to teach, share, warn about, celebrate?
- What does writing your story mean to you or your business? How do you feel about that? What is driving you to do this?
- What does your perfectly-crafted story look like?
- Think about holding that book in your hands. How does that make you feel?

Hold on to this thought and feeling—this joy and exhilaration is why we create. It's why we write and share our stories. It's also why we read.

Weave your spells. Share your magick with the world. Be brave and confident—and enjoy the journey.

ABOUT THE AUTHOR

Founder of Fae Blood Publications, Ruth Fae is an intuitive writing coach and editor, international bestselling author, youth mentor, and chief editor at the Women Writing Intentionally Collective. A believer in the unlimited potential of co-creation, she works in energetic flow with her clients to break through their writing blocks, release their stories from their heads and hearts, and confidently share their message with the world.

Through her years as a journalist and copywriter, Ruth has learned that the true magick of storytelling is to heal, nurture, and create connection through sharing the wisdom of our experiences. A rebel at heart, she loves to challenge convention as a coach, speaker, and mentor within the world of indie publishing.

An avid lover of the performing arts, Ruth is a columnist, reviewer, and editor for *Dance Writer Australia*. With a keen interest in encouraging the voice of our younger generations, Ruth values her years of experience writing for *Indigo*, a unique and empowering magazine for teenage girls.

More recently, she has shared her stories about life, writing, and the power of communication on *Medium*; the *I Wrote That*, *Lunar Life*, and *Life Stories Unscripted* podcasts; and in the Women Writing Intentionally Collective community.

Residing in Melbourne, Australia, Ruth Fae shares her 'life of love and magic' with her partner, their blended family of seven children, and an adorably naughty puppy named Merlin.

Connect with Ruth:
- ➢ Email: ruth@faebloodpublications.com.au
- ➢ Website: faebloodpublications.com.au
- ➢ Instagram: @fae_blood_publications
- ➢ LinkedIn: linkedin.com/company/fae-blood-publications
- ➢ Facebook: facebook.com/faebloodpublications

Chapter 8

How Book Coaching Helps You Write Your Best Book

by Erin R Lund

Writing a book is a lot of work that can feel like a slog, but it doesn't have to feel that way. When you work with a book coach to write your book, you'll get an experienced guide who will lead and encourage you through the process. She is a project manager who keeps track of your progress and work left to do, an accountability partner who ensures that you stick to a writing schedule of regular writing assignments and due dates, a knowledgeable editor who understands the literary landscape to help you see where your book best fits into it, a publishing expert who helps you decide how you want to publish your book and create a publishing plan, and a cheerleader who encourages and supports you every step of the way by bolstering you when you flag and celebrating you when you reach your writing and publishing goals. She is your personal book coach, a co-pilot, and collaborator on your author journey! She is me.

I'm Erin, a book coach and developmental editor for writers of life-changing books that share meaningful transformations, whether through self-help, memoir, alternative spirituality, or holistic wellness. I help experts, educators, and entrepreneurs write books to teach and inspire others with their stories and expertise. As a coach, I am a helper, and I love working with those in the helping professions of personal development, nursing, counseling, social work, body work, holistic healing and wellness, spiritual guidance, education, and life coaching of all kinds who aid in supporting the physical, psychological, intellectual, emotional, and spiritual well-being of others. I work with both novice writers seeking to publish their first book and seasoned authors seeking to level up their writing to help them become thought leaders in their industries and fields of expertise. I am especially passionate about elevating women's voices and stories with my coaching and editing work.

When considering writing a book, think through what you'd like your published book to do for you. Many writers today are publishing books to position themselves as leaders in their fields and to offer their expertise to a larger audience. Becoming a published author elevates visibility, reach, and authority, which helps experts, educators, and entrepreneurs build their brand and grow their business to create a life of prosperity and freedom. For women especially, writing and publishing a book can help create paths to freedom that we've not had access to in the past.

Writing a book is a revealing process which can feel unnerving; however, when you dig deep within yourself to find your true voice, the one that emerges from your authentic self in your soul, writing a book is a liberating process. Too often, many of us have lived lives based on what certain others or society think constitutes an ideal life, rather than living from our soul's greatest joy and desire, which dearly wants to be known and expressed. Other people and circumstances can quash our soul and its voice, and whether done intentionally or not, the result is that we do not truly know ourselves because we do not fully feel ourselves, so we cannot fully express ourselves. This quashing of our soul affects us on every level, even though we may not realize it, which leaves us feeling numb and frustrated.

Digging deep into the ground of your being unearths your authentic voice, which liberates your soul to sing its song and bring its gifts to the world. This is what the desire to write a book is—your soul's burning need to speak and be heard, to share what it knows to be true. This is digging up your treasure and giving the gold of your voice to the world to bring this healing power to others who need your guidance, to help them feel the inspiration that authentic voices impart, and to encourage them to do the same work for themselves. Books give us wings, both when we write them and when we read them!

Because writing a book may be a new process and experience for you, let me show you the Master Plan book coaching process I created to help my clients outline, organize, and write books through using some key tools I developed so you can gain clarity on your book and write it with confidence and ease. Each tool is designed to build on the previous one to guide you gently and methodically through the process of fully developing your book's concept, arc, and form.

Doing this structural work also helps you do all of your thinking, planning, and organizing work first, so when you sit down to write your book, you can move right into the flow state needed for writing and use your developmental work as roadmaps to guide you in writing your content.

You can begin by clarifying your book's foundation and progression by working through the simple steps of this Five Keys exercise. Answering the questions in this exercise as thoroughly as you can helps you gain clarity on the following components of your book:

1. *Key transformation.* What major transformation does your book offer your readers? From what undesirable state to what desirable outcome, for yourself or your readers?
2. *Key message.* What is the main idea or key concept of your book? What is its primary message for your reader?
3. *Key reader.* Who are you writing this book for? Who are they in the world? Who would most love to hear your message and undergo your transformative process?
4. *Key genre and market.* What genre does your book best fit in? In a bookstore, it can only sit on one shelf. What is the label on that shelf?
5. *Key transformative process.* What are the before and after stages of the transformation your book offers, and what are the stages in between them that take the reader from the former to the latter?

Knowing these five keys will provide you with immediate clarity and confidence to begin your author journey. The first four keys are like the four corners of a building's foundation, and the fifth is like laying the floor that takes your reader from its front door to the back door, where they walk out transformed and step into a new life.

The fifth key also provides the essential shape of your book to help you begin organizing it, from your book's opening with the undesirable state you or your reader are in, through naming each stage of your transformative process, to your book's final outcome state at its end. In this way, you can see the shape of your book in a single snapshot and assess and adjust its clarity, organization, and flow as needed.

After you complete the Five Keys exercise, you can begin developing the stages of your transformative process into specific concepts and accompanying action steps. Each named concept and its step will then become a chapter in your book. To do this, create an Annotated Table of Contents, which is not only a list of your book's chapters, but also includes a brief summary of each chapter's intended content. Begin by listing each step in your book's transformative process, and write a few sentences describing each step's main theme and specific stage of inner work for your reader to do. When completed, this document will then create another snapshot of your book, with a bit more detail, to help you assess how each chapter speaks to and flows into the others to ensure a logical and coherent reading experience for your reader.

Once you have determined your book's overall structure and are satisfied with its organization and flow, you will be ready to deepen your developmental process by organizing the intended content of each chapter using these tools: a Chapter Template and Chapter Outlines. These tools ensure that you include vital elements in your chapters and that these elements are presented in a logical and organically fluid format that easily leads your readers through your content.

This Chapter Template contains what I feel are the vital elements of prescriptive nonfiction books like self-help and personal development, in what I feel is the most logical order to present them to best capture and maintain your reader's interest. Using a chapter template also creates a consistent experience for your reader through each chapter, as they come to understand what to expect from each one, and this consistency carries them through the book like a steady rhythm, like a heartbeat. Consistency is reassuring, especially when feeling frazzled and frustrated by the unwanted circumstances and feelings your reader is experiencing that draws them to your book seeking validation, education, inspiration, and transformation. These are the vital chapter elements, in order:

1. *Transition A.* In each chapter after the first, this element provides a brief transition from the last chapter's key concept and transformative step into the next chapter's key concept and transformative step, so your reader understands the logic of the progression you are taking them through.

2. *Introduction.* This element introduces the chapter's key concept, then discusses why it is relevant to your reader, how it fits into the book's theme, and where it fits into the transformative process your book is sharing.

3. *Exploration.* This element delves into how the chapter's key concept and step in your transformative process particularly help your reader, which may include statistics or information from other sources, and bring them closer to their desired outcome.

4. *Illustration.* This element shares how the chapter's key concept and transformative step have helped you and/or selected clients of yours (shared with permission) by presenting one personal story—either yours, a client's, or one of each—to illustrate the key concept and how this chapter's step works to move your reader through your transformative process.

5. *Integration.* This element presents any relevant exercises, journal prompts, worksheets, meditations, affirmations, etc., you may have to help your reader process and integrate the information presented in the chapter.

6. *Conclusion.* This element wraps up the chapter by briefly restating the chapter's key concept, its step in the transformative process, and how this step helps the reader achieve their desired outcome. While this is presented in the chapter's introduction, these concepts will be much clearer to your reader now that they have read through the chapter, so it is a good idea to reiterate the chapter's key concept and the importance of its transformative step.

7. *Transition B.* This final element transitions your reader into the next chapter by describing how the key concept and transformational step in this chapter naturally move into the key concept and transformative step to be presented in the following chapter, so your reader will understand the logic of your progression and feel enticed to turn the page and keep reading.

After studying this template, use it in tandem with the content you wrote in your chapter summaries in the Annotated Table of Contents to create Chapter Outlines by writing brief summaries of what content you want to present for each element of each chapter of your book. The outlines will then contain everything you intend to include in your chapters so you can write your book with ease!

You can use the same process to write your book's Introduction by utilizing an Introduction Template and Outline to help ensure you include the key elements every Introduction should contain and present them in a logical and fluid way. These key elements are as follows:

- The problem your book discusses, which is what your reader is likely experiencing and no longer wants to
- The solution, or the transformational process you are offering your reader, which will lead them to what they want to be experiencing
- Proof of the solution, as your personal experience or a client success story
- Who you are and your particular position of authority for writing about your book's topic and presenting its transformative process, such as being an expert in the area you're writing about or someone who has experienced this problem and found a solution that worked

- Who the book is for
- Who the book is not for
- An orientation to the book's progression in a brief overview of either the steps of the transformative process you are presenting or the book's content chapter by chapter
- Your personal reason for why you wrote this book
- What main lesson you want your reader to take away from reading it

Now, if you're reading this and feeling that it looks like a lot of work, well, you're right, it is. But don't be discouraged! I created these tools and processes to help writers understand, simplify, and move systematically through the process of planning and organizing a nonfiction book because I am not only a book coach, but also a book author, and I encountered some blocks I hadn't expected when I wrote my book. *Who knew you could feel so frustrated and blocked when also feeling a burning desire to share a message that you understand so well?!* I didn't.

And that is actually the reason you will likely run up against this block: because you understand your message and transformative process *so well* that it makes *perfect sense* to you in *your* head. But something happens when you excitedly sit down to write it out—you realize that you aren't sure how to present and discuss this in the kinds of ways and words that will ensure your message will readily make sense to *other people* in *their* heads! Gah! This was a block I hadn't expected, and it stopped me in my writing tracks. I had to backpedal my writing to focus on thinking through and pinning my concepts and steps to the page so I could see them; only then could I begin to clarify and organize them into a logical and beautiful structure, which I could *then* fill in with my writing.

These planning and organizing stages and tools are designed to help you sort out this hard stuff in digestible steps which then become clear roadmaps that guide you in writing your book with clarity, confidence, and ease. I want you to successfully write a book, and I want you to *enjoy* your writing process! Book coaches help you do both. *With a book coach, you don't have to struggle alone to write your book like I did when I wrote mine.*

I also learned that to successfully write a book to completion, it is imperative to create a writing schedule, as one of the most vital elements of writing any book is ensuring you will have the time to write it. Don't leave your writing time to chance or happenstance: you need dedicated time for writing, and on a regular basis. You must carve out the hours you'll need and schedule them. You know what happens when you don't? Life. It will nearly always take precedent. You have to prioritize and protect your writing time to ensure you'll actually write and complete your life-changing book. It's not optional, it's critical, and this was true for me as well when I wrote my book.

Examine your schedule and find an hour each day for six days of the week, ensuring that you also take a day off to rest and refresh yourself. That hour doesn't have to occur at the same time each day, but it does need to exist, and you do need to protect it.

When you find those hours, write them down and pin them up where you and your household can see them. Your writing schedule must be sacred, not viewed as expendable time you can borrow for other, more pressing matters. Devote yourself to a daily writing practice the way a monk dedicates herself to daily prayers. Create your personal writing space and make it pleasant and inviting with whatever inspires you, like plants, candles, crystals, music, or motivational quotes.

Once you have scheduled and commenced your writing, track both how many words you produce in an hour-long writing session, and how many hours it takes you to write a chapter. You can then use this data to project how many more hours you'll need to finish your book and forecast a completion date. Seeing your estimated finish line keeps you energized and motivated, which helps you complete your book.

Through utilizing key tools like these with the guidance, encouragement, and accountability of a book coach who is invested in your success, you will have what you need to write your best book!

I also support writers as an editor by offering a variety of editing services for completed manuscripts. Manuscript editing is done in four key stages that progress in order from wide-scope concerns to narrow-scope concerns, which refine the manuscript through each stage of editing. Some editors specialize in just one stage of editing, and some editors are trained in and offer all these stages.

THE FOUR STAGES OF EDITING, IN THE ORDER IN WHICH THEY ARE DONE:

1. Developmental editing, which assesses and advises on the overall structure, flow, and clarity of your manuscript, and the same within each of your book's chapters.
2. Line editing, which creates stronger and smoother writing by assessing and advising on passive sentences, weak verbs, vague or confusing phrasing, verb-noun disagreement, problems with tense, misplaced modifiers, and industry jargon that won't be familiar to your reader.
3. Copyediting, which corrects grammatical errors of spelling and punctuation.
4. Proofreading, which ensures your final copy is as free of any grammatical or formatting errors as possible to ready your manuscript for publishing.

Writing a book and becoming an author is a journey that takes you both into yourself and out into the world. A book coach can help you dig deep to find your soul's true voice, plan and organize your thoughts, and provide you with editorial expertise to guide you in writing your best book. I find my work as a book coach and editor to be fulfilling and rewarding, and truly an honor to help writers share their powerful truths with others. The world needs your wisdom and guidance, so let your soul sing it!

Happy Writing!

ABOUT THE AUTHOR

Erin R Lund is a nonfiction book coach and developmental editor who owns Sunshine Editorial Services & Book Coaching, where she helps experts, educators, and entrepreneurs write life-changing books to teach and inspire others with their stories and expertise.

She offers book coaching packages and editing services that help writers create a master plan for their books, propose and pitch them, write them, and polish them for publication. She specializes in the genres of self-help, personal growth, memoir, alternative spirituality, and holistic health and well-being. She works with both independent and traditionally published authors.

Erin has been spotlighted online in interviews by Jess Kotzer of Self Pub Hub, Laura Hernandez of Spiritual Female Entrepreneurs, and the Books, Bards & Ballads series presented by the Sisterhood of Avalon.

Under her pen name, Erin Aurelia, Erin is the author of *The Torch of Brighid: Flametending for Transformation*, published by Moon Books Publishing. She has also been published in anthologies by Moon Books and Goddess Ink Press.

Additionally, Erin is a poet who has composed three poetry collections: Bone & Stars, Love Conspiracy, and Feral. In Spring 2021, Erin served as the managing poetry editor for *VoiceCatcher,* an online women's literary journal in the Pacific Northwest. She has performed her spoken word in several open mics and regional shows, where she is known for her dynamic and powerful style.

Erin is a mother of two grown sons and lives in Vancouver, Washington, with more books than she can read in this lifetime. Find her downtown performing her poetry in open mics and shows, accompanied by her favorite local musicians.

Connect with Erin:
➢ Website: sunshineeditorialservices.com
➢ LinkedIn: linkedin.com/in/erin-r-lund
➢ Facebook: facebook.com/erinbookcoach

Chapter 9

Ghostwriting
A Solution to Your Writing Excuses

by Terri Tonkin

At some time in your life, have you ever considered writing your own book?

Let me guess what emotions and feelings came up for you.

Fear. Anxiety. Overwhelm. *I'm not good enough. Nobody would read it. I don't have time. Where would I start? How would I start?*

Your head and heart were in a spin.

I know. I've been there.

Let me share with you what it was like for me in the beginning, and how I am now living my dream.

Writing my own book had been a dream of mine since I was a little girl. I grew up in rural Queensland, Australia, and we didn't have a television until after I had started school. Even then, it was limited viewing with two, maybe three stations to choose from, and only for a few hours a day. Sounds like I grew up in the dinosaur era compared to what is available today.

I spent a lot of my time outside playing or being with my dad, working on cars or in the yard. My favourite time was when I could lie on my bed and read a book. I have always had books. I loved reading.

I would read the Enid Blyton books, *The Secret Seven, The Famous Five,* and others. *Anne of Green Gables, Pollyanna,* and many more became my best friends. At school, in the early years, I loved the library. I became a member of the local library, so I always had books to read.

Over the years, I have lost count of the number of books I have read. When my mum passed away recently, I found a trunk filled with the books I had read as a child. If only I had known my parents had kept them, they would not have been in the condition they were. They would have been preserved for posterity.

Each time my husband and I have moved, I've done a purge of my books, as we would run out of storage space. I have read so many novels, I have to keep passing them along so as not to overfill my bookshelves.

As the years went by, I developed a strong interest in personal/professional development. Again, I have purchased so many books in this genre, it is hard to part with any of them.

I truly am addicted to books.

The addiction took a turn in 2018, when I decided to write my own book. It was the realisation of my childhood dream. I spoke to a mentor and told her it was time. She asked me, 'Why now'? The answer was quite simple: I had run out of excuses.

I was no longer working full-time. I had just completed a coaching course. I was in a financial position to do so. My mum's health was deteriorating, and I wanted her to be able to read my book before she passed. I wanted to leave a legacy for my grandchildren. I had more reasons to write my book than not.

Since writing *My Time to Shine*, I have contributed to 15 compilation books. I had caught the bug—the writing bug.

I only wish I had caught it earlier in life. I had found my passion.

I saw a post on social media related to ghostwriting. It piqued my curiosity. I had a vague idea, yet had never done any research around it. I started following a group on Facebook, and my curiosity increased. I registered to attend a free training, and it changed my life.

I understood the training would take about an hour. The facilitator was still presenting at two hours, then almost three hours. He took the time to respond to questions, provide additional information, and best of all, was not salesy or pushy. I was hooked.

I signed up for his paid training and have not regretted it or looked back. Through this training, I was provided the tools required to turn my love of writing into a business, where I would be paid for doing what I love to do: write.

Within a month of announcing it to the world (because if it's on Facebook, it's real, right?), I signed my first ghostwriting client to complete a manuscript. Within 12 months, I had signed my third client.

Through connections and networking, I have gained clients for varying opportunities. For some, I have completed résumés. For a travel agent friend, I wrote some travel blogs. A web designer has engaged me to do some content work and some article rewrites. Author friends have engaged me to review their books and assist with rewrites.

I am based in Australia, and I have had local, interstate, and overseas clients. Ghostwriting has opened up the world to me and for me.

Enough about me for now. Let's return to you wanting to write your own book, and perhaps why you haven't.

Research quoted in the *New York Times* shows that 81 percent of people surveyed have thought about writing their own book. And while it's a lot harder to quantify, some online sources suggest 97 percent of people who start writing their book don't complete it.

It is interesting to me that, if that figure is accurate, only 3 percent of those who start to write a book actually complete it. And not all of those completed will be published.

There are numerous reasons, or excuses, for this phenomenon. One of the biggest is time. *I don't have enough time. I have other commitments. My family is my priority. I'm too busy.* And I'm sure there are many other iterations of the 'time' reason.

Many people carry a belief that no one will want to read their story. *It's boring. It is only my story. Someone else wrote a book and it didn't sell.* Again, various reasons around beliefs.

It could be that they don't feel they have the skills to write a book. We all have to start at the beginning every time we do something new. And the beauty of this industry is, there are beta readers, proofreaders, editors, and book coaches available to assist.

An alternative to writing your book or story yourself is to engage a ghostwriter.

In basic terms, a ghostwriter is a professional writer who is hired to create a written manuscript or piece of work on behalf of another person. They reflect the ideas, intentions, and vision of the 'author' (the client). The work will be written in the voice of the client, who becomes the author of the completed work; they own it and can use it however they wish. The ghostwriter is compensated for the work completed.

Generally, the ghostwriter isn't acknowledged for the work, unless the author wishes to disclose their involvement.

Ghostwriters may be used to write manuscripts, blogs, newsletters, social media, and web content. Some ghostwriters do copywriting as well. There are many written pieces completed by ghostwriters for varying mediums. Think songs, screenplays, manuals, and online programs.

Who is it for? Anyone who wants written content and has a myriad of reasons as to why they cannot complete it themselves has the option to engage a ghostwriter.

Not all ghostwriters are the same or offer the same services. Pricing will vary from price per word to price per project. Services provided could be written work only, through to a full package including writing, editing, publishing, and marketing. It is important to note, the more services provided, the higher the cost will be. Each element in the package requires compensation.

My preferred genres are memoir, lifestyle, well-being, and business. Nonfiction is my forte. I have not yet delved into fiction, though there are ghostwriters who do.

When approached by a potential client, I want to get to know them. I need to know why they want to write a book, the purpose of the book, and how it will help them in their business. I arrange a one-to-one meeting, in person, if possible, or via Zoom. This meeting provides a wealth of information and will determine if the client and I can work collaboratively together.

For each discussion I have with a client, I record the session to ensure I have captured information I require to complete the work and any arrangements or agreements we may have discussed for the duration of the engagement. This protects my client and myself.

If we agree to work together, I provide a copy of my agreement to the client, which details the scope of work agreed to, timelines, payment details, the expectations the client is to meet, and those I am required to fulfill. When this agreement is completed, dated, and signed by both parties and the first payment has been received, the work will begin.

Completion times are negotiable, within reason. If the piece is 1,000 words, it would be a matter of days. If a manuscript of 40,000 words is required, the timeframe could be within six months. If a large piece of work is required within a tight timeframe, the cost may be higher.

Once the first chapter of a book is completed, I will forward a copy to the client for feedback. This ensures I am capturing their thoughts, vision, and voice. It is important to do this, as it is their story, not mine.

I set regular times to catch up with my clients, whether it be weekly or fortnightly, to gather additional information and to provide a progress report of my work. This may be face to face via Zoom, telephone, or email. The regular exchange of information ensures the content and context are meeting the needs of the client.

I price my work according to what I am requested to do. For a manuscript, I charge a flat fee; the higher the word count, the higher the fee. If I am doing a review/rewrite, the fee is priced per word. Again, not all ghostwriters use the same pricing method. My payment terms are usually one-third up front, mid-project, and a final payment on completion.

This is usually for a larger piece of work. If it is a 1,000-word piece, full payment is required on completion of the project.

Ghostwriters can completely write the manuscript/document, or the client can write the work and the ghostwriter does a review and potentially a rewrite. There are options.

The timing of each project is negotiable. The minimum for a manuscript is four months, however I have had a client complete their 30,000-word manuscript within three months. Another extended out to almost six months. I allow for flexibility, for as we all know, life can get in the way of the best-laid plans. However, I would not like to see a project drag out for too long.

The project is a collaborative effort, and each party must be willing to discuss any matters arising, with an agreed outcome of having the best possible work presented. When I receive feedback from the client, I amend and adjust where required. It does not mean I will do endless edits. If seeking a change, the client would need to be able to express the reasoning behind the change, and how it would improve the desired outcome. This is where some people (generalisation here) believe that, as the 'author', they get to have unlimited changes, without explanation.

The author is a paying client who has agreed on scope, payments, and time. The client may review the work provided at any time during the process and at completion. When the final draft is agreed upon and approved by the client, it is ready to be passed to the next stage, e.g., editing or publishing.

With my business model, I write the manuscript (or piece of work), and I hand that work back to the client. The author decides if, when, and how it is to be published. I am not in the publishing business— not my forte. I provide my clients with a list of editors, publishers, and marketing gurus. I have many other connections to whom I can refer my clients for the services they require.

Some ghostwriters offer package deals, with all the services needed included. Their fees will reflect the additional services, as in some cases, those services are outsourced and need to be paid by the ghostwriter, who passes those costs to the client. Other ghostwriters may offer a range of services, yet not all that is required. Each client needs to do their own research as to what services they require.

The client may only need the writing services and decide to self-publish. They may require some services and not others. The client is the best person to decide which services they need. As a ghostwriter, I can guide them and/or refer them to others to complete the journey. The journey is theirs to have.

I have many connections and I am a regular networker. The majority of my clients have been referred to me via my connections. Not everyone who requires the services I offer will become my client. Some will, some won't. I recently had a referral come my way, and after an initial discussion for a rewrite, we decided I would do the first chapter to see if my writing style suited them and would meet the needs of their ideal reader. I completed the first chapter; they weren't sold. We had another meeting, and I completed another version. After a week had passed, they emailed to say my writing style was not what they were seeking and they were going to engage a copywriter. I found this interesting in that a copywriter is very different to a ghostwriter. However, writers can, and do, do both.

Not everyone is going to like my style, just as I'm not going to want to work with everyone who is referred to me. I prefer to work with people who are open to feedback, collaborative, and passionate about their work. Having said that, I believe my life journey and experiences have made me a better writer.

Whilst writing for the compilation book, *Forever Changed by Suicide*, another contributing author asked me if I would be interested in collaborating on a book she was compiling on domestic and family violence. I declined, as I felt I could not write with integrity on the subject, as I have been blessed to not be subjected to this.

Then my first ghostwriting client approached me to write her story. I had met her through my networks, and she felt she knew me, liked me, and trusted me. She was a survivor of domestic and family violence. Okay, Universe, I'm getting the message. It was a steep learning curve for me, but I was able to write her story and not be triggered emotionally. And it was therapeutic for her to release her story and trust me to write it. I assured her that she was in a safe place, as was everything she told me, which I kept confidential. I asked her to speak to her solicitor, as there were legal proceedings outstanding. I had her check with her therapist, as she was still under treatment. Until those issues were addressed, I didn't want to proceed. They all gave the green light to go ahead.

Upon completion, my client thanked me, as releasing her story had made her life a little easier. She had shared what she'd experienced and the pitfalls of the legal system. She wanted others who found them-selves in similar situations to know what lay ahead for them and how they could work through the issues.

My second client was a domestic and family violence survivor. She wanted to share her story as an educational tool for organisations and churches to understand the stories of victims, the help they needed, and how to navigate the legal system.

My third client is an intuitive healer. She wants to share her story, as for many years, her wisdom, knowledge, and abilities were sup-pressed. She is reclaiming herself and wants to share what she knows.

All stories are different, even though they may have similarities. Each story told and shared will have an impact on another person. Storytelling can be informative and educational. We can share facts, beliefs, perspectives, and experiences. It will always be our own story, yet by sharing, we can help others.

I am passionate about serving others by helping them explore their own beliefs, values, and perspectives, identify their potential, and reclaim a part of their lives. I utilise their experiences combined with my skills and knowledge to understand their needs and desires.

Ghostwriting matters to me, as I get to do what I love to do. I am able to provide a service and opportunity to those who wish to become an author, yet don't want to do the writing for whatever reason. It is important for potential clients to have this resource available to achieve their dreams and goals. They can share their stories and help others by doing so.

Telling a story can be therapeutic and healing, and the impact of sharing stories is far-reaching. It lets others know they are not alone, and not the only one who has been in a similar situation. Stories provide hope. Stories build connections. And through connections, your network will grow. You will find like-minded people. Your community will grow.

Everyone has a story to tell. Most people have more than one. If you want to write a book and have a list of excuses as to why you can't, there is a solution to each one. Go back to your 'why'. How will your story impact others? What legacy will you be leaving?

Ghostwriters have the time. They have the experience and the expertise. They will work collaboratively with you to achieve the outcome you desire. If they are not able to provide the suite of services you need, they have connections they can refer you to.

Back to my original question:

Have you ever considered writing your own book?

How many reasons do you have to not write your book?

Let me help you tell, write, and share your story.

ABOUT THE AUTHOR

Have you ever wanted to write your book and share your story?

Terri Tonkin knows how this feels because as a child, she always wanted to write her own book. She achieved this dream at the young age of 60.

Terri is now a multiple international bestselling author, ghostwriter, and life coach. She has written her own book, contributed to 14 compilation books, and is now writing manuscripts for others.

Terri has been featured in *The Corporate Escapists* and *Disruptive Publishing* magazines and has been interviewed on *Voices on Fire*, *Empowered to Shine*, *Fast Forward Your Entrepreneur Journey,* and *The Corporate Escapists* podcasts.

She is the face of Connect Within, and her clients are heard, validated, acknowledged, encouraged, and supported to find the solutions they are searching for.

Terri aspires to inspire the people she meets to reach their potential, as inspiration leads to motivation and motivation leads to action, providing results.

Her life has been a journey of ups and downs, trials and tribulations, both personally and professionally. She is a lifelong learner and avid reader who seeks out new opportunities and loves to travel.

Connect with Terri:
- ➤ Facebook: facebook.com/connectwithinmindsetlifecoach
- ➤ LinkedIn: linkedin.com/in/terri-tonkin
- ➤ connectwithin.com.au
- ➤ Email: terri@connectwithin.com.au

Chapter 10

How to Choose the Ideal Editor

by Dragonfly De La Luz

If you came to this book because you want to be a writer, good news: Anyone can write! But not everyone can edit. And any writing intended for publication needs an editor.

Writing, in its most basic sense, is putting ideas to paper. It doesn't necessarily have to be artful or poetic, it only has to get a message across. Generally speaking, writing is subjective. Editing is not. (Well, it *can* be. More on that later.) Editing has hard and fast rules that many people assume they know intuitively. After all, most of us speak English every day of our lives—how hard could it be to edit English text?

You'd be surprised. Editing the English language, with all its complexities and exceptions to rules, is far from intuitive. What may pass as acceptable in speech or informal writing can come across as unprofessional—and challenge your credibility as a writer or publisher—in the realm of formal writing, where most books exist. Moreover, the rules of grammar are fluid; there are volumes upon volumes of style guides that are continually being updated to reflect the evolution of language in modern society, and the only way to know what is correct these days is, frankly (boringly), to study them.

Unless you've got a penchant for reference books, any style guide will likely make your eyes glaze over after about two minutes. But if you're a total editing nerd, you eat this stuff for breakfast, lunch, dinner, *and* dessert.

Hi. I'm Dragonfly. I'm an editing nerd. I'm obsessed with creating a frictionless reading experience that ensures professionalism and credibility for writers and publishers who don't really geek out on editing. And over the course of this chapter, I'm going to tell you all you need to know to choose the perfect editor for your project.

First, some background on why you can trust my expertise. I did a double-major in English and Women's Studies, which is also when I got my start as an editor, and studied Social Justice in graduate school, around which time I became a regularly published writer. But I didn't go to college to get a job; I went to follow my passion. I never expected that following my heart would actually prepare me for a career—indeed, *be* my career—yet here I am, a solid 16 years into professional life as a writer and over 20 years as an editor. I spend my days doing what I love most: editing and ghostwriting in the genres of memoir, self-help, personal development, business, and spirituality. (I also edited this book.) I have become one of the fortunate few whose passion pays them.

And what is my passion, exactly? It goes beyond just editing, and so does my work with writers and publishers. My passion is starting with a writer's rough draft and alchemizing it into something truly magnificent: powerful content that shines and makes an unforgettable impact. My passion is creating instant credibility for indie publishers by ensuring their books are properly and professionally edited so they can attract high-caliber collaborators. Truthfully, it is more than a passion; it is the gift I was born with.

As an indie publisher, when you approach potential collaborators about contributing a chapter to your multiauthor book, you can be assured of one thing: they are going directly to Amazon to examine your previously published books. And they won't just be looking for the wisdom and inspiration they impart. Any potential collaborator with a writing background is looking to see if having their name attached to your project will build their reputation... or hurt it.

Someone who is not a writer and is simply excited for the opportunity to tell their friends and family that they're a published author may overlook typos and other editing faux pas. They may not even catch them. But a talented writer, one with the skill to elevate your book, absolutely will, and may turn down your proposal to collaborate on that basis alone.

Publishing a multiauthor book is not just a chance to shine a light on the stories of people who might otherwise never share them. It's an opportunity for you to build your reputation and credibility as a publisher. Multiauthor books naturally lend themselves to errors and inconsistencies because instead of editing just one writer's style, there are a dozen or more that have to be checked for consistency not just within each chapter, but across all chapters. A properly, professionally edited book that is free of typographical, grammatical, and formatting errors will attract talented writers whose contributions will create clout for your publishing company, which will then attract more talented writers, creating a virtuous cycle that continually elevates your books and your brand.

Of course, not all indie publishers have a background in writing or editing, nor should they have to; just as most writers and editors don't have the know-how to turn a book into an international bestseller. Publishing at its best is a collaboration of multiple people who know and excel in their own zone of genius. You don't have to be a trained editor to be a successful publisher, you just have to hire one.

My work has evolved to become a fluid, highly specialized hybrid model of multiple editing modalities combined with true-to-you ghostwriting that maintains your vision and honors your voice. But it requires much more than mere editing acumen.

HOW TO CHOOSE THE RIGHT EDITOR

Any good editor will check for inconsistencies, underdeveloped ideas, and unclear arguments. A great editor will provide you with feedback on how to make your writing more compelling, develop your ideas in a more sophisticated and nuanced way, and stand out from the competition, by suggesting sentence or entire section rewrites with step-by-step instructions.

But even a great editor might not be the best editor for you. Clear instruction usually works fine for people who have innate editing and writing skills, but simply telling an aspiring writer who's not an editor what they need to do to improve their writing is analogous to a mechanic telling you what to fix in your engine and sending you on your way. Although this could work for someone whose goal is to perfect their craft and master the art of writing, for someone who simply wants to get a manuscript ready for publication, that style can lead to endless frustration, unnecessary overwhelm, and precious time wasted.

After years of honing my expertise across the spectrum of editing— from developmental editing to line editing, copyediting, and proofreading—I have refined and adapted my practice to meet writers' and publishers' needs far beyond the standard correction of errors and guidance on improving their writing. I endeavor to understand my authors and their projects on such a deep level that not only can I execute most rewrites for them myself, saving them untold hours of time and exasperation, but I do so in a way that emulates their voice and elevates their writing to result in a piece that is gracefully coherent and polished to perfection.

Most editors focus solely on the text in front of them—an approach which suits many skilled and experienced writers just fine. But for those with no formal training in the art of writing or editing, that approach may get them little more than grammatically correct sentences that still don't convey the message their hearts yearn to share. For many indie publishers, or aspiring authors who know what they want to say but don't know quite how to say it, a more holistic approach is necessary.

Rather than focus only on the content, I gain a complete understanding of the project and the writer's/publisher's goals before ever editing a word. This way, I can dive into the document in a manner that enables me to enhance their message and edit seamlessly in their voice. One of my favorite—and most frequent—compliments is that my edits mesh so perfectly, the authors often can't tell where their writing ends and my editing begins. This, to me, is the sign of a job well done.

For many writers and publishers, particularly those not endowed with refined editing skills, this level of editorial versatility is the unicorn, the ideal scenario. But no matter how talented an editor I may be, that doesn't necessarily mean I'm the ideal editor for you. And finding the right editor for your project is essential.

KNOW WHAT KIND OF SUPPORT YOU NEED

The first step in finding the ideal editor is knowing what kind of editing/writing support you need. It's not as cut-and-dried as you might expect. You would think that in a profession that prides itself on precision, there would be clearly defined, universally agreed upon terms. One of the ironies of editing is that this is not, in fact, the case.

There are subtle nuances in the definition of all levels of editing that leave plenty of room for interpretation, so it's important to come to a shared understanding of your editing needs up front, so the editor knows exactly what is expected of them.

Many people assume an editor's role is at the end of the writing journey. But contrary to popular assumption, there are four main types of editing relevant to the various phases of the writing process.

Developmental editing (also content or substantive editing)

When you're in the early stages of writing a book, whether you have a rough draft or just a rough idea, a developmental editor will make sure you're conveying your message clearly, even to those unfamiliar with the subject matter.

Developmental editors take a substantive look from front to back, checking overall structure, recommending or even executing section rewrites, restructuring outlines, and ensuring flow within the book as a whole and within each chapter. They have the skill to overhaul and evolve your work, which can be especially helpful for those who have their ideas intact but lack clarity on how best to organize them.

If you're ready to tell your story but have no idea *how* to tell it, a skilled developmental editor can help you flesh out, organize, and develop your ideas, as well as find and refine your own authentic voice, which is of particular importance for memoirists and multiauthor books.

Line editing

After the work has undergone a developmental edit, a line editor polishes the language, ensuring consistency of style and tone.

Copyediting

Once the project has been polished, a copy editor fixes any grammatical, mechanical, or factual errors, ensures correct punctuation is used, and handles all the nitty-gritty components around proper usage of the English language. Written English is not as intuitive as spoken English, so a trained, professional editor (preferably with an English degree) who is familiar with all relevant and updated style and grammar guides is essential.

Proofreading

When you've completed the manuscript and need a final pair of eyes to catch typos and formatting errors before publication, a proofreader with an exceptionally keen eye for detail meticulously ensures you've dotted all your i's and crossed all your t's, so your project is professional and spotless.

Ghostwriting

Even if your intention is to self-publish, if you're not a seasoned writer, it's important to recognize your limitations regarding the written word. If you have a fervent desire to tell your story but lack the skill to artfully convey it, you might consider hiring a ghostwriter to help you get it on paper. Ghostwriting is more common than you might think, and for good reason. It allows people with great ideas but not much writing ability (or great writing ability but not much time) to hire a professional to transform their ideas into a completed manuscript.

For memoirists, this can be especially helpful. One of the most efficient ways to write a memoir is for the author to simply tell their story—literally—while the ghostwriter records and transcribes it. Sitting for an interview may bring out your story much more naturally than writing it, and a skilled ghostwriter will know what to ask to get at the heart of the themes and complexities that make your story unique. This arrangement works particularly well if the ghostwriter is also a skilled developmental editor who can organize key life events into a compelling narrative and ensure the written version of the story flows well within a solid structure.

Pro tip: Editors are paid per word, per hour, or per project. You can save yourself time and money by self-editing as much as possible beforehand.

One of the most revealing ways to do this is to read the entire piece out loud. This process can highlight the parts that need to be reworked for clarity, readability, and rhythm.

Now that you have a better understanding of the editing and writing support you need, what should you look for in choosing the right editor for your project?

CHARACTERISTICS OF THE IDEAL EDITOR

Every editor has their own strengths, and one who excels at copyediting may not have the same talent in developmental editing. But your ideal editor would be skilled in *all* of these categories—every editing modality plus ghostwriting—enough to walk with you each step of the way and see your publishing journey through to fruition.

The ideal editor is one with a diverse background, who can draw from multiple styles and genres to help you communicate and connect with your audience. As a former academician with an eccentric, spiritual upbringing who's lived or traveled all over the planet, I have always walked in many worlds. Having such global life and academic experience means I can craft and edit in language that is uber-technical, deeply spiritual, super stylistic, culturally colloquial, or, truly, whatever the project calls for. One of my specialties is making content shine even if English is not the writer's first language. And, having done my graduate work in Social Justice, I can help writers employ conscious and inclusive language where requested.

Your ideal editor is a *trained editing professional* (not just someone who's "good with words") who will make sure nothing stands in the way of you achieving the credibility you've worked so hard for. She is more than just someone with the skill and expertise to elevate your writing to a level capable of impressing agents, publishers, and your audience (or future clients); she is someone who resonates deeply with your work and truly understands your vision.

It is crucially important that your ideal editor be able to prove their expertise. How? References are helpful, but what you'll really want them to provide are actual samples of their editing ability. Specifically, ask to see original documents as they were *before* they edited them and the final version they returned to the client *after* they edited them (with client permission, of course).

The reason this is so necessary is because, unfortunately, many people call themselves editors even though they have no formal education or training in editing. Writing can be intuitive; editing is certainly not. You wouldn't choose a surgeon whose only qualification was that they attended a webinar on how to perform heart surgery, would you? Nor should you risk the credibility of your book by hiring an editor who is not formally trained.

As a professional who has been hired countless times to re-edit documents and manuscripts for clients who were unsatisfied with their original "editor," I can assure you, the difference between a qualified editor and a hobbyist is glaringly obvious. But there's no need to go into the editing process blind to the quality you can expect.

If your potential editor can't provide any previous work samples, the next best way to determine if they're right for you is simply by giving them a straightforward, low-commitment shot at editing your work. Hire an editor for a trial edit, with a predetermined block of time of anywhere from two to four hours. This way, you can see for yourself if you resonate with their comments, suggestions, and editing style, and whether they are truly capable of taking your writing to the next level before you commit. And shop around. Feel free to request samples and trial edits from multiple editors before you make a decision.

A writer's relationship with an editor is built on trust and collaboration. You're seeking someone you can trust with your "book baby" that you've carried and nurtured for months, if not years, and may be introducing to the world for the first time through this editing relationship. Trust is required not just in terms of competence and skill, but as regards the editor's ability to respect your relationship with your book and communicate about why they recommend certain changes in a way that honors you and your project. So it's important that you resonate with their communication style. Put another way, it helps if you actually *like* your editor. You'll be working together closely, so finding someone who's highly skilled *and* whose energy elevates you will smooth the process infinitely.

Rather than judge you for what you don't know, the ideal editor will be your biggest cheerleader and will take the time to understand your vision, message, and audience to elevate your writing to the very best it can be. But while your editor won't judge you for typos and grammatical mistakes (we recognize that not everyone shares the same demented passion for the English language that we do), your readers and potential clients certainly will. If your writing has errors or poor grammar throughout, you risk undermining your credibility and having readers dismiss it before they ever get to the parts that make your story impossible to put down.

Even to the casual reader, errors are a red flag that the writer may not be as skilled or professional as they claim. If they see one, they start looking for others. And the more they see, the less they trust you as a writer. They wonder what else might be wrong with the piece and begin to doubt that it will deliver. Just as damaging, seeing these mistakes creates friction, and that friction pulls them out of the story, ruining the immersive reading experience.

As an editor, my primary goal is to create a frictionless reading experience. Although identifying and correcting errors is important, so much of editing is not about what's right or wrong, but rather what will cause the least friction for readers. The ideal editor eliminates distractions caused by confusing or awkward phrasing, but also recognizes the difference between errors and preferences. My job is to find ways to make the writing as smooth and digestible as possible, even if it means deviating from strict rules of grammar or syntax, because, indeed, the ideal editor will know the rules well enough to know when—and how—to break them.

Finally, your ideal editor understands the need for editing to be a collaborative process and never forgets who's in the driver's seat. You always have the final say about what changes to apply to your work, full stop.

Even the most talented writers benefit from the fresh perspective an editor brings. No matter how keen their attention to detail, there will always be things a writer can't see when they've become too close to their own work to view it objectively. A skilled outside editor is the most assured route to a final product that is polished, professional, and capable of making a lasting impact.

Writing is messy. Publishing can be overwhelming. But you don't have to be a naturally talented writer to sound like one. Whether you're writing a solo project or publishing a multiauthor book, a gifted hybrid editor can be activated at any stage of the process to make an inexperienced writer sound like a professional writer and make your best work even better. I'm here for it! And I'm here for you, supporting you and cheering you on start to finish.

ABOUT THE AUTHOR

Dragonfly De La Luz is a writer and editor, as well as author of the forthcoming book, *The Manifestation Experiment*, a spiritual travel memoir about her three-year solo journey manifesting her way around the world.

She has a BA in English and editorial expertise that spans the spectrum, including developmental editing, copyediting, and proofreading. From seed and concept to polished manuscript, she brings over 20 years of meticulous editing and professional writing experience to bear in helping publishers and aspiring authors turn their writing dreams into pinch-me reality. With her uncanny ability to write and edit in each writer's unique voice, she has a particular passion for editing multiauthor books.

As a journalist and copywriter, Dragonfly has written for diverse clientele against the backdrop of some of the most inspiring vistas on the planet as she explores the world as a digital nomad. She is the editor of *Shadows of Atlantis, Book One: The Awakening* and *Book Two: Symbiosis*, among many other indie projects—including this book, *Get Published: Industry Experts Share Their Secrets*. Her work has been featured on *National Public Radio (NPR)*, published in *Huff Post*, and mentioned in *Newsweek*. Her articles can be found in numerous magazines, she has written for television, and she is a frequent contributor to online mind-body-spirit publications.

When she's not laser-focused on editing, Dragonfly spends her time cultivating love and enchantment with her manifested soulmate. Her side hustle is her soul's calling: coaching women to manifest the one they want or alchemize their relationship with the one they're with.

Since almost all her clients come through word-of-mouth referrals, she doesn't use social media to promote herself professionally. But you can still follow her tantalizing life of world travel and epic romance!

Connect with Dragonfly:
- ➤ Website: dragonflyediting.com
- ➤ Email: dragonflydelaluz@gmail.com
- ➤ Instagram: @Dragonfly_Manifests
- ➤ Facebook: Dragonfly De La Luz

Chapter 11

Editor's Magic
Tips and Tricks Towards Publishing Success

by Serena Scarlett

INTRODUCTION

There are lots of ways to be a successful writer, like finding a style that works for you and receiving feedback. Most of all, be interesting. Captivating content is vital.

With experience editing several multiauthor books as well as solo author projects, ebooks, and marketing materials, I bring you many insights. They are designed to accelerate you from a blank page to a completed manuscript.

Experienced editors can tell you what *not* to do. For example, don't get hung up on sticking to a particular style; you can find your own.

They can guide you in helpful technique, developing your style, and improving engagement for the reader. In this chapter, I will impart much of this to you, along with methods for intuitive writing, finding your creative flow, and the nitty-gritty must-dos of editing. Finally, I will provide information on how launching your book can promote your business. My suggestions may surprise you, as I challenge some of the expected or traditionally accepted rules of writing.

Writing brings you gifts. There is an exquisite exchange in both giving and receiving. As Mary Gooden from Divine Destiny Publishing says, 'Writing is the gift that just keeps on giving'! The process and outcomes may surprise and enchant you. Many say getting published is a portal to wonderful opportunities and advancing in personal growth.

Writing and editing are my hobby business. My main work is as a therapeutic counsellor (therapist). I love being a good listener, providing empathetic problem-solving, and exploring options to life's challenges. We all need a professional, an expert in a field to give us objectivity. Being close to our own situations, we sometimes can't see the way forward. Similarly, in writing, we can get too close to it. Others need to review it objectively. What may be interesting or important to us as a writer may be boring to a reader.

ENGAGING READERS AND AVOIDING BORING CONTENT

A captivating read is vital. You won't necessarily start an article just talking about your own life. Others aren't that interested. Or are they? If you have a story that many others can relate to, by all means share it. But do it in a way that engages, entertains, or enthralls.

One way to help a reader relate to your story is to offer a similar tale to what they may have experienced. Include solutions they may need. Think from your reader's perspective. Do they really want to hear your arduous journey, challenges, or problems? Probably not.

They are looking for solutions to their own issues and ways to make their journey in life smoother. To draw them in, state early on what the reader will gain.

The aim is to inspire your reader to think, *Yes, that's me. The author knows all about this. They have insights I can benefit from.* Your journey may have gems of wisdom you can give to others. Ideally, your writing will lead up to those gifts, providing answers, solutions, or new ways of looking at life.

Bear in mind that people are usually time-poor. Try not to waste their time. Keep the content on track and interesting. Avoid repetitive or unnecessary words. Repetition of an idea is acceptable if you are illustrating a point. When you do that, it's helpful to preface it with, 'As I mentioned earlier'. Keep your paragraphs concise and related to one main theme. And it's easier for your reader to take things in if your sentences contain just two to three bits of information.

The reader needs to feel satisfied. Finish with a punchline that is profound, enlightening, or provides a sense of completion. People investing their time to read your work need to be rewarded. Ensure it is worthwhile and that they gain something from it.

Re-read what you have written. Check it over to ensure it clearly describes what you want to impart. But it's important not to get bogged down in this stage. Write, write, write. Fine-tuning can come later. Relevant and interesting content is what's most important. Again, to engage a reader you must keep them enthralled. Be adventurous and expressive. Use descriptive words in bite-sized chunks that are easy to digest.

Let's consider styles. People's styles can be sticking points, where they overthink and labour over things such as whether to write in first- or third-person. Just write, see what comes, and don't limit yourself.

It is helpful to explore what writing guidelines you need to stick to and what can be considered creative license. The best tip I ever learnt from an editor was that styles can be mixed, and there is no specific style you must use. You may discover your own. Don't you love that freedom? The key is to keep creativity flowing. In fact, start with that.

I can't overemphasise the importance of getting the words down, however they come. Let what is natural come onto the page. We can get too caught up in sentence structure and grammar, stifling the flow. The grammar is best done after large chunks are down. Always ask a colleague, friend, or paid professional to edit your work. We can get too close to our work to pick up mistakes and inconsistencies.

My best tip? Be yourself! Give yourself permission to discover your own self-expression. This may bring a unique writing style or process. You may surprise yourself and come up with something amazing. Instead of being concerned if you are writing well enough, forget the rules, at least to begin with. For now, simply enjoy!

EDITOR'S MAGIC

Once your ideas are written, then comes the process of editing. For me, when the author submits their piece, I start with comprehension. Does the work make sense? Is it engaging and portraying points clearly? In the developmental stage I am focused on continuity, with sections being in an order that is easy for the reader to follow. Avoid too much repetition and long, unsatisfying sentences. It can give the reader an unpleasant experience.

That said, sentences that are long and poetic may be the writer's style. I once edited a piece with sentences of four or five points down to two or three. The author told me they felt their voice was lost. I revised, editing with less verve, and allowed their style to remain. They said they loved it. And I was reminded that there are many wonderful styles.

Editing is a fine balance, a combination of assistance in creating what is correct in overall writing terms and maintaining the author's creative purpose. Our shared goal is keeping it enjoyable for the reader. One of the biggest challenges I face as an editor is not enough consideration for the reader and their perspective. Sure, you are writing from your perspective, but ultimately, if the readers don't like it, you're failing.

After the writing and the editing comes the challenge and satisfaction of publishing your work. To be successful is a combination of being read and liked by many, as well as (hopefully) wide distribution and sales.

Multiauthor books have special features leading to success, including the benefits of a wide network. The authors promote the book collectively so that your chapter has exposure to more readers than if you undertook it alone. This means more people, more readers, and potentially more clients for your particular endeavour. You can choose the genre or topic of a multiauthor book and join with like-minded writers in a collaborative project.

WRITING INTUITIVELY

In my last two multiauthor books, I wrote intuitively, and in one I described how to do this. If you also have a spiritual leaning, perhaps you can give it a try.

> *There is a place, a voice of wisdom and inspiration waiting for you somewhere near. You move towards it and let it come to you. This action has an open, active intent with it, a little like allowing the next person to speak in a conversation.*
>
> *What will you hear? What will you write?*
> —Serena Scarlett, *Aligned Leaders*

Your essence, the spirit of your vision, needs to shine. It's simple to do by not only using your own vast experience, but also imbuing your writing with inspiration from 'The Source'.

When you write intuitively, a topic may come, or just a few simple words. Intuition has a gentle, quiet voice. Listen. Allow. Then write whatever comes. You may draw a whole manuscript in.

Richard Bach said his first book, *Jonathan Livingstone Seagull,* came to him as an intuitive 'download'. It's a timeless self-help book that has many gems of truth and wisdom.

Writing with intuitive flow is a way that I enjoy very much. Other writers use a variety of methods for the way they translate information. Play with methods yourself. You may be nicely surprised!

Spiritual content or messages reported to have come from origins other than the writer's mind can come forth in the process of intuitive writing. These messages, or downloads, can come through automatic writing, channeling, or accessing The Source. In this form, the author is not usually intent on providing their own opinion, but rather what they have sourced as truth or meaning.

One manuscript that I edited was completely written from a download. It had incomplete sentences and virtually nonexistent grammar. This was due to the flow of the author in simply getting down the content without interruption. It's a good plan to do that—get the main content down, then edit the wording and grammar later.

Reading content directly from automatic writing would be difficult to understand. The meaning may be obscured due to the manuscript requiring a lot of developmental editing. However, having a spiritual background myself, I was familiar with the content's overall meaning and purpose.

What worked for me as an editor in polishing the manuscript was knowing the topic so well. Being an eclectic, spiritual person, the content of the download was familiar to me. This may sound strange due to it being another's work, but I came to see that the meaningful and wondrous content that had come from the open mind of the author was actually universal truth. Truth is.

From the edit, the grammar was corrected and sentence structure improved. It became a brilliant self-help book that I highly recommend, *Awaken the Creator Within: Ascend to Your Higher Reality*. It is packed with practical ways to move forward in life and can be found on Amazon.

For this manuscript edit, being an expert in the field was paramount. This is an important point. A good editor must know their subject. I would not take on a job for a technical manual or ebook on the features of using Excel spreadsheets. I baulk at number-crunching. It's simply not my thing.

My work centres around editing helpful and meaningful guides for life written by changemakers with a spiritual inclination. I enjoy working with people who are intent on making a difference in the world and provide a pathway for others to follow.

True stories are fine too, so long as they are kind. Many share their own story to offer others encouragement to persevere through trials and tribulations.

> *Truth doesn't alter, although your perception of it may vary or alter greatly.*
>
> —John and Lyn St Clair-Thomas

What aspects of your truth are you portraying? Your story may be true for you. But is it also true for others you are writing about? A word of warning: When you write about abuse, domestic violence, or situations involving others, it's important to consider legal aspects. What you write may be true for you. Perhaps it's a true account of how you experienced it. However, the other party will have their story, their experience, and it may vary from yours. You could leave yourself open to legal liability, so it's best to consider carefully what you say about others. Changing their name is not enough. If it can be interpreted that the work is about them, you leave yourself vulnerable. I suggest getting legal advice; it's beyond my experience other than to caution.

Offending others in autobiographies can also be a trap if sensitive situations are exposed that others can be upset by or just want kept private. One way around this is to get permission first. Share what you write about the person and get their feedback before it goes to print. That way, you can consider changing or omitting it. And if you keep it, at least you will know what may come from doing so. Forewarned is forearmed.

Having others read your work is imperative. We are too close to our own writing to pick up what needs changing. However, I always recommend the author do a final proof. After all, you are putting your name on it, so it reflects on you. The meaning of what you publish needs to represent you accurately. Some editing can inadvertently change meaning, so it's important to do a final read of the whole.

Mistakes may slip through. This is not the end of the world. When I was training in copywriting for marketing purposes, my teacher provided a useful tip. If you have a typo, know that not all customers will be put off. It shows you are human, a real, living, caring, if imperfect, soul; not some super slick impersonal company out to fleece the reader. In that way a mistake can go in your favour.

That said, editors are important to polish your work, as they provide professionalism and increase respect for you in your field. After all, being published provides a platform that elevates you amongst those in your field. It can be a launch pad for greater success.

PROMOTING YOUR BUSINESS WITH YOUR BOOK

To be published in a book can give you instant credibility. This is due to a few factors, one being the longstanding respect for the talent that is required to achieve writing a book and getting published. The other is demonstrating your expertise. After my first book was published, the feedback was incredible. 'Serena, I see you are doing so well now'! 'You have a book'!

Launching a book, or even re-launching, can be a powerful marketing tool. Many authors utilise being published to promote their business. Ideally, the purpose of this needs to be considered before you start writing.

Who is your target audience? Which people need the solutions in your book? What problems do they have and how does your writing help them find answers? Returning to my earlier advice, load your chapters with juicy, easy solutions. Fill your reader with hope that they have found someone they can trust. Do this by providing all they need on your topic. Give value, be generous, and offer all the wisdom you have gained. Share it. Give away your secrets. They will love you for it and come back to you when they want to engage someone. Why? Because they got amazing benefits from you already, and you are an expert in your field.

If you are in business and writing about your services, it's a good idea to provide a call to action. Do this toward the end of your article or chapter. Lead up to an action you suggest the reader take. This might be going to your website and getting a freebie or subscribing to your email list for tips and tricks.

A pal of mine, Julie Nelson, published an ebook on her specialty of wellness via aromatherapy. She created a set called The Fragrant Oracle Cards with stunning images depicting aromatherapy flowers. Her ebook that accompanies the set is brimming with beautiful healing solutions for life. Just for subscribing to her newsletter she offers a freebie on how to use essential oils for well-being. It's an excellent example of a call to action and giving value to your potential customers. Once a customer is linked to you, then you can offer them more. In Julie's case, she offers an amazing range of uplifting, unique healing services.

As a counsellor and therapist, my work is a healing service too. It helps others to live happily and be true to themselves, getting around the challenges that come to them. I love my work. All that I have done over my life has led me to this moment of being the best I can be, so that I am there to help others be who they want to be. Success in me is success in you.

When you know that you are the creator of your life, that spirit and spark are bountiful and limitless, there is nothing you can't do. By dreaming, setting goals that are both large and small, and being enthusiastic for life and living, you can create a path that is both fabulous and fulfilling.

Writing can offer so much to the reader—healing and guiding them, providing answers that give relief from long-term problems, feelings of uplift, and so much more. What do you want to impart? How do you wish to influence your reader? Guide them. Make their life better. And if you have a goal of engaging more clients, your readers will naturally want your energy, your special touch.

Share your stuff. Shine through your words with genuine, gorgeous, gratifying goodness. Be game to allow your personality and self-expression to burst from the pages. Be exciting. Be you. And feel confident that a good editor will keep that flavour, tantalising the reader and leaving them wanting more.

ABOUT THE AUTHOR

Serena Scarlett is a 'spiritual wordsmith' who recognises magic and draws on the natural order of life. She infuses truth and healing into her written and spoken work. She is deep, wise, and wistful.

Serena enjoys many roles. She is an accomplished author, editor, and mentor to entrepreneurs. In her work as a therapeutic counsellor, Serena imparts gems of wisdom with outstanding results. Problems vanish and pathways open up.

Serena brings to her work the following:

➢ Wise counsel and spiritual gifts
➢ Therapy, counselling, and business mentoring
➢ Well-being and natural therapy options
➢ Extensive studies and competencies in spiritual development, including magic and manifestation
➢ Manuscript editing and dazzling copywriting
➢ Oracle card creation
➢ Creative writing and healing
➢ Global business mentoring, including in the US, Europe, and Australia

Serena graduated from university and found purpose and meaning in helping others via counselling and editing services. Her accomplishments demonstrate the wisdom she's gained from navigating life's challenges and include the following:

➢ International bestselling author, 2021 – 2023
➢ Published in *Recovery Poets*, Summer 2020
➢ CREA Brainz Global Award-winner, 2021 – 2022 (awarded for creative ideas and writing to support mental health)
➢ Senior Executive Contributor for *Brainz Magazine*, 2022 – 2023

Serena lives near Sydney, Australia, with her partner and beloved pets.

Connect with Serena:
➢ scarlettcreativ.com
➢ Email: spirit444@gmail.com

Chapter 12

Navigating Your Choices in Publishing

Be Like Water, Find Your Creative Ocean, and Swim

by Mary E. Gregory

I was bonked on the head when I realized I needed to be a writer. At no other time in my life had I been told, and in no uncertain terms, you must write your memoir and you must be a writer. But how I got there was unexpected and super inconvenient.

I'd been looking for a direction to take my creative pursuits. I didn't know exactly which direction I wanted to go, but I did want one. I'd shared my personal story with many people in my life. Each time, someone would tell me, "You should write a book!" I'd hear that and think, *Yeah, yeah.* But in the back of my mind, I thought maybe I should. But do I know how to? Could it really be a book? After a few attempts to write my story, dribbling out a chapter or a paragraph at a time, I really had no clue as to what it would take to write my life story, let alone how to get it published. But soon enough, I would not only self-publish my memoir, but begin the journey to traditional publishing.

I was 36 years old and feeling at a crossroads in life when my author journey began unexpectedly with me not getting a job I wanted.

SOMEONE GRAB A PADDLE, I'M GOING DOWN SHIT'S CREEK!

I was offered a position that would allow me to pivot from my role as an admin of a time-keeping system to one that I really wanted in product management. Since this was an internal opportunity, I decided I would prove myself a bit and do parts of the job before they offered me the role, to show I had the skills. No one asked me to do this, I just felt I should.

After about three months, the moment came. I walked into the meeting knowing the position would be offered at a certain salary that would be exactly what I wanted, that I would blush, humbly accept their offer, and set a start date. However, this isn't exactly how it went down.

The hiring manager offered me the job, to which I replied, "Why, yes, thank you! What will the salary be?"

"Oh, well this would be a lateral move for you; there's no salary increase."

"Meaning, no increase in my pay?" I asked.

"Yes, that's correct. We didn't think that mattered to you. You have been working on specs for the past few months. We thought you just wanted to move into the role," she said.

"Yes, I want the new role, but I also want to make at least $20k more than what I'm making now. I was performing the role because I wanted to prove to you that I had the skills, not that I didn't want to make more money."

The hiring manager looked puzzled. In her defense, I never told her that my intention was to make $20k more per year for the new job, and she never asked me to put in work to prove myself before she would extend the offer. I just expected her to read my mind.

After the crushing realization that this lateral move was not at all what I had telepathically communicated to the hiring manager's mind, and knowing I would not take the job without the raise, I quickly told her, "No, I won't accept. The salary is not what I want."

"Well, I can't get you that amount," she responded, "but maybe half of that."

"No, it's this amount or nothing."

"Then I guess we'll rescind the offer."

Oh, shit.

I'd said too much at this point and could not recover. As the year ended, I could hear from my cubicle the team I should have been on, wrapping up their successes and talking about how next year's challenges would bring them closer together. All the while, I knew I should be on that team, and if it wasn't for my stupid outburst, my lack of ability to set expectations, and this feeling of inadequacy coupled with always having to prove myself, I would be sitting with them right now, feeling quite content. *What the hell is wrong with me?* I thought.

CAN I GET A SLICE OF HUMBLE PIE? I DON'T MIND IF IT'S $200/HOUR

Sometimes it's experiences like these that set us down a path of personal discovery, one where we think, *Where did I go wrong? What could I have done differently? Can I make a change?* The answer is always yes.

So I began opening up to others about my disappointment and asking for advice. I decided that I'd be open to sharing my missteps and hearing from other people how they think I could have done things differently. And I would be humble.

As I did this, a whole world of advice came at me, and each recommendation became little rivers of insight. I chose to think of them as places where I could put my boat and ride them 'til the end to see what wisdom I could glean from them. I could also decide to hop off when the advice didn't feel right. But I was open to receiving wisdom.

And when I truly opened myself up, I was led to my creative ocean. It was vast and precarious. It was turbulent and majestic. I decided to swim in it.

My first stream was a podcast called *Serial.* It hit on my personal love of crime stories and got me to pay attention to storytelling in a way that was not visual. The arc of each episode laid out tidbits of information that allowed the listener to go on a journey, to make their own judgments. I loved this medium.

On another podcast I explored, I heard from a man named Hal Elrod. He'd recently released his book, *The Miracle Morning,* and his story was so inspiring that I bought the book later that day.

Hal's Life S.A.V.E.R.S. resonated with me. The premise was that for one hour a day, before your workday starts, you focus on dividing 10 minutes of personal development across six areas: Silence (Meditation), Affirmations, Visualization, Exercise, Reading, and Scribing (Journaling). Two streams led to a new river. If you don't have a morning personal development regimen, his book is the best way to get started. It was just what I was looking for to change my habits, perhaps to change my opportunities at my company too.

Being that I'd never been a morning person, the morning soon became magical. I'd never carved out time for myself like this and I looked forward to getting up early. I was always pulled into the current of life, very "go with the flow," but I quickly realized I have a lot of control over my time.

I enjoyed the quiet of the morning hours, as it gave me the space to think and reflect, to learn and recharge. It had a profound impact on my life almost immediately. It was just a few days into this practice that I decided to write my memoir, and two weeks later, I decided to quit my job.

The Miracle Morning suggests you reach out to 10 of your closest friends and family, maybe even an ex-, and ask them, "What do you see about me that's getting in my own way?" What came back was profound and helped lay the foundation for my new journey. One person said that I gossiped too much. Another person said I allowed others to take control over my life and then I'd lash out when things didn't turn out the way I wanted them to. In all the feedback I got, I saw truth.

Most of us don't ask our closest friends and family to give us feedback about ourselves, especially with the agreement of no possibility of recourse. Maybe this should be something we all do every 10 years. It's amazing to see what others think about you but would never share unless asked. We all have blind spots, and my friends and family were in awe of my vulnerability. I took my own personal feedback to heart to write my story. And then I set out on one of the most interesting journeys of my life, one of personal transformation, one that led to therapy at $200/hour.

I KNOW I'M MOVING, BUT WHERE AM I GOING?

My life at the time was not what I wanted. If I didn't address my childhood trauma (and, let's face it, my adulthood trauma), I'd never get anywhere with this personal transformation. So I stopped resisting the work I'd have to do and just leaned in.

I spent 30 days laser-focused on what would get me moving in a new direction. I started to get clarity and focus. I learned how to express myself and ask for what I wanted, versus expecting others to know what I wanted, and I started to discover my voice. I started writing my memoir. Oh, and in this time, I landed a new role at my company making exactly $20k more per year.

Soon after I started writing my memoir, I received an email from Hal promoting his group dedicated to self-publishing. This group walked you through how to write your book, provided a community of other writers, and encouraged the collaboration of authors. It also shared insights into the inner workings of the publishing business and advocated for a path to self-publishing. I signed up.

WHAT IS YOUR WHY?

For some, being an author is a stepping stone to selling courses or consulting services, or it's simply about having the respect of being a published author. But for many, it's none of these. It's just to share a personal story and heal from it.

To find your "why" helps focus your intentions and, ultimately, find your creative ocean. Mine was to share my personal journey and inspire others, including myself. I really wanted to examine why I was in the boat I was in and find a way to overcome my past limitations, which were really my present limitations. I wanted to change the narrative

I'd been holding onto, the one that said I was not smart enough, capable enough, experienced enough; the one that kept me from sharing ideas and navigating ambiguities in the face of fear. I didn't want to be adrift any longer. I wanted to tap into my full potential.

All this wandering got me into the therapist's chair to talk about my issues. It was work, and it was not easy work. It was hard, ugly-crying work. Work that you don't discuss at work, either. But it was good work. It was *the* work. The deep, soul-searching, life-affirming, bad habit-clearing work. The work that I do to this day. Not just because I Marie-Kondo'ed that one scary closet, but because I'm doing that for my entire soul.

I found the ability to forgive myself and others by going through EMDR treatment, an experience I share in my memoir. EMDR (eye movement desensitization and reprocessing) is a form of psychotherapy that enables people to heal from the symptoms and emotional distress that result from trauma. I had big trauma. After processing that trauma, I was able to show up differently in the world. I was able to recognize the impact it had on my life, and I didn't have to carry that with me when I showed up in my personal or work life any longer. My work and personal life began to improve dramatically and it gave me the courage to pursue the big dreams I'd had but left in the closet for fear of failing.

WHY I CHOSE TO SELF-PUBLISH

The world of traditional publishing seemed more difficult to enter than self-publishing, at least at the time. Self-publishing felt like the fastest route to get my work out there, and it didn't have to be perfect. I needed to feel more in control and to build my confidence as a writer. Self-publishing showed me that I was more than capable of doing it on my own.

I signed up for Hal's 90-day self-publishing program to take me from blank page to published author. I was jazzed, enthused, and utterly unprepared for the journey I would be on. The program was excellent, and though it took me five years to write my book, there's no doubt in my mind that one could, and many have, become published authors in just three months. This just wasn't me.

I was someone who was still defining who I was. Still scared to call myself a writer. Still unsure of how this program would impact me. I felt like I had jumped into the sea of choppy waters and was wondering what the hell I was doing there. But it was the best first leap I could have taken into the world of publishing.

Among many other things, the training instilled the value of having an accountability partner. Having someone holding you accountable for steady progress towards your writing goals is important. My first accountability partner became my book cover designer. Although she published her book almost four years ahead of me, I grew so much from committing to a writing goal each week and checking in to hold myself accountable. Throughout this process, I learned the value of reading your book aloud and hiring professional editors, formatters, and book cover designers; doing research on your target market; copyrighting your work; researching and finding the right categories to publish in; and having a launch team. All these things mattered. And the community was so critical to my success as a writer. I had found a tribe.

FIND YOUR TRIBE AND CLAIM YOUR TIME

I'd never pursued personal dreams while holding down a full-time job and didn't realize how stressful this can be, especially if your expectations aren't tempered accordingly. When we think of writing, we usually think of it as a one-way street; we write, and that's it. But a lot of writing is about learning from others, reading other books in your genre, and, of course, taking time to write and get feedback on your writing. Determine what space and time you have to dedicate to research, creativity, musing, and feedback.

I prioritize writing on personal or collaborative projects most days, but some weeks are focused on research and reading. It's important to give yourself time for experiencing each aspect of the writing craft.

Some weeks you will have more time for writing and some weeks you're going to be pulled into other areas of your life that aren't part of your creative craft. Finding that balance is always a goal and not a means to an end. You're learning and growing, and that takes time. Your experiences always end up in your writing somehow, so give yourself grace for some weeks not ending up like you planned. Life is what happens when plans fail.

Writing my memoir was extremely triggering. I had to get my personal house in order. This took years. I had to grow up a lot, and my maturity as a person expressed itself through my writing journey. I'm proud to say that my debut memoir, *Travels Through Aqua, Green, and Blue*, is an expression of that journey, and I am forever grateful for my willingness and bravery to pick a direction. I'm a better writer and it's a better book because I didn't rush.

MY JOURNEY TOWARD TRADITIONAL PUBLISHING

This is the creek I'm drinking from now. I'm currently writing the second draft of a nonfiction book about forgiveness. I've found my tribe through Pitch to Published, a community of dedicated professionals who have set a high bar for writers. They guide you to find the best literary agent for your writing career and hold your work to the professional standards expected of the literary community.

If you choose the traditional publishing route, you'll need a good pitch, a bonding open, an amazing query letter, and in some cases, a finished manuscript. You'll also need a rock-solid proposal that breaks down your marketing plan and shows that you're going to be a partner with your literary agent, you have the right audience, and you have put in the work to grow and nurture your readers.

What I've learned about going the traditional publishing route is that as a debut author, you have an opportunity to put out your work without some of the industry's expectations of proven success. You're able to pitch your work as a future bestseller, and depending on how good your pitch and manuscript are, they just might believe you. Because you've never been published, the possibilities are endless. It's like you're this little golden egg that your agent gets to crack. Think about being the uncracked golden egg when you consider which path you'd like to take, as you'll only be a debut author once.

When I self-published, I did not know about this prized title of being a debut author and the leverage it would have given me. I thought it was just the opposite, that there was no chance that an agent would want to represent me if I was a nobody. That couldn't be farther from the truth.

Since this chapter is about sharing my experience, I should say that had I not been so concerned about proving myself, so concerned about my legitimacy of being a "writer," I would have considered going the traditional publishing route and used my first book to my advantage. If you happen to know now that you want to be a full-time writer one day, or you have a manuscript that's completed and you feel confident in your work, I'd suggest considering going the traditional publishing route for your debut book.

ANTHOLOGY OPPORTUNITIES

I have been part of two multiauthor books and the benefits have been extraordinary. I've networked with incredible people who were from varying professions and in different phases of their writing career.

What I've found to be so great about these opportunities is that you're part of a community of people going through the process of publishing *together*. Some may be at the very beginning of their writing career and not quite ready to publish an entire book on their own, and some may be professional writers wanting to contribute to a book that has a subject matter they've got extensive experience and expertise in.

In my case, it's been important to grow my network, collaborate, and rejuvenate my passion for writing my second book, *Forgiveness Deficient*. I've found that co-authoring anthologies has been just what I needed to spice up my writers' tribe and get new ideas and insights from other creatives and business leaders. I wanted the thrill of writing and publishing a book and being held to a deadline, but without having the weight of the entire marketing and publishing process on my shoulders. I also wanted to have a bestselling book under my belt, which I was able to achieve. It has brought me great pride and helped boost my confidence.

As you can see, there are many reasons to be part of this type of publication, and this may be the right start for you.

MY BEST ADVICE

When you're ready to take the leap into writing a book, find a program that's right for you, one that provides you with practical advice and a balanced, approachable way to develop an actionable plan to publish your book. No matter what stream you choose to lead you to your creative ocean, know that you will learn and grow and become a better person—and better writer—for choosing a path and pursuing your dreams.

If you're willing to put in the work to move from fantasy to reality, what better way to do that than being in control of how you tell your story? Water always finds a way. Dare to find your creative ocean, and when you do, just swim.

ABOUT THE AUTHOR

Mary E. Gregory is a bestselling American author, poet, and memoirist. She is a senior IT leader at a Fortune 500 live entertainment company in Los Angeles, California. She leads her team by encouraging their pursuit of personal passions while having a work life. Mary's philosophy is that people are happier, more satisfied, have livelier conversations, and more opportunities to build and nurture relationships when they're actively pursuing their dreams. She has been featured in *Entrepreneur Magazine* and on the popular podcasts *Too Opinionated* and *The Future Is Human*.

Mary is a passionate and heartfelt leader who infuses her writing with humanity and realism and possesses a deft and balanced approach to storytelling. Her stories are about resilience, forgiveness, transformation, and the human condition.

Her debut book, *Travels Through Aqua, Green, and Blue: A Memoir,* won best first line by BookLife, a Publisher's Weekly company, and was endorsed by Stan Wlodkowski, the executive producer of *Eat, Pray, Love* and *Arrival*, as well as international bestselling author, Hal Elrod.

Mary was born in Nashville, Tennessee, and is the youngest of three. She is a proud #catmom of several feline muses. She holds a degree in Management Information Systems from California State University, Long Beach. She is also a member of the American Society of Composers, Authors, and Publishers (ASCAP).

If you want to feel inspired and uplifted, follow her journey online.

Connect with Mary:

- ➤ maryegregory.com
- ➤ Instagram: instagram.com/maryegregoryauthor
- ➤ Twitter: twitter.com/MsMaryEGregory
- ➤ Facebook: facebook.com/maryegregoryauthor
- ➤ Email Mary for speaking engagements and interviews at info@maryegregory.com

Chapter 13

Don't Skimp on the Cover Art

by Kristina Conatser

If people don't notice your cover or connect with it, the author of the book next to yours will be grateful.

—David Leonhardt

Within the ebbs and flows of your manuscript is a message, a valuable story to share with your audience; a captivating and connecting string of words which will draw on the emotions and inspirations of your readers and heighten their insights. But how does it reach them?

Marketing is a highly valuable tool that is vital for positioning your product for visibility. For books, one of the most important pieces of marketing is your book cover. When a consumer strolls through a bookstore or scrolls online, your book has around 15 seconds to capture their attention. Your cover design is the first thing the consumer will see, and, contrary to the adage, people do judge books by their cover art. It's important to make that first impression count.

Your cover art tells your story through visual design. It reaches your audience in a way words alone cannot. It gives the reader an initial feeling of the purpose of your book. It captivates them and fuels them to want to read further. Or not, and your potential reader scrolls along to the next book.

Over the last few years, I have seen a large uptick in new authors taking the leap to get their story out there. And as diverse as their stories may be, they all need the same thing: a captivating book cover.

As a graphic designer, my passion is bringing my clients' visions to life through creative design. Every cover art piece is unique and challenging in its own way, and each project gives me the opportunity to do a deep dive with my clients to learn about their story. Hearing an author share what their story means to them gives it so much life and passion, helping me to zero in on the important elements that should be focal on the cover art.

I believe the story is yours, so you should have some input on the result. Your story is personal and important to you, so how it comes to fruition should be just as intimate a process. You've poured your heart, knowledge, and time into your manuscript. Skimping on cover design does such an injustice to all your hard work.

> *I've learned that people will forget what you said, people will forget what you did, but people will never forget how you made them feel.*
>
> —Maya Angelou

More and more, people are enjoying the exploration of designing their own covers, and if you've got a great eye for color, image placement, and balance, it can turn out great! Designing a cover for your book is fun and highly creative, but it's easy to get caught up in the colors and all the fonts and end up with something too overwhelming. We live in the age of DIY, and many want to do it themselves to save a dollar. But often, doing it yourself can turn into a mountain of stress for someone who doesn't specialize in this field. Hiring a graphic designer to take care of those tasks for you allows you to focus on what you are most passionate about. But if you decide to take a turn at DIY cover design, here are a few mistakes you should avoid:

- *Too many fonts.* When designing a book cover, the rule of thumb is to use no more than two font styles that pair well together.
- *Illegible font styles.* Your book cover should be able to be read from a distance, so the font needs to be large enough and clear enough to be eye-catching near or far. Decorative fonts are fun to look at but are very difficult to read for many consumers.
- *Too much clutter.* Less is more. It's great to have many ideas for your cover, but try not to put all those ideas in the same concept. Your book cover should have a healthy balance of negative space, design elements, and text.
- *Improper text placement.* When designing your cover, your text should not be near the edges. This will risk your text being cut off during the printing process. The most effective way to prevent your text from going into the cut lines or bleed zone is to utilize a cover art template that is adjusted for your book's trim size. These can be found on many printers' websites.

Whether you are a DIY cover creator or you're hiring a graphic designer, it's important to know that you will have different file types for each format of book publishing. For an ebook format, your final cover design file output will be a JPEG in RGB color model, and it will be front cover only. For print, you will receive a press-ready file, often in PDF format, which will feature the front, back, and spine.

Your book cover is not a part of the publishing process to skimp on. As you've probably gathered by now, there is much more to cover design than placing an image and some text on a page. It is a creative process that should be in alignment with your book's genre, be attractive to your target audience, and pair well with your story.

The graphics should be well thought out, match the genre, and make sense. Text design should be well balanced, properly sized, and legible. Graphics used without the proper permissions and licensing can land the author in heaps of legal trouble or lead to their book being pulled from shelves. Furthermore, if the overall design is done poorly and the book is unable to captivate or connect with the target readers, it will result in a loss of sales, leaving the book to collect dust.

Another key component of making sure your book reaches its intended audience is the title. If your title is too long, the text can overwhelm the overall design, drawing attention away from the beautiful visual design elements.

If you do decide to hire a professional, finding a graphic designer that knows and understands your book genre, asks you questions about your project, and maintains healthy communication is key. A graphic designer who doesn't invest in the informational side of your project will not be able to provide a quality design that effectively depicts your book.

In the same way that you should never skimp on your cover art, you should also never settle for just anyone to design your cover. You run the risk of receiving a finished product you're not happy with if you settle for a designer offering something quick and cheap. This is your story: invest in it. Don't be afraid to hold others to the same accountability. Everyone involved in your project should be passionately investing their time and skill set to provide you with the best end product you can have.

There are a few key things a graphic designer should know about book cover design before accepting your project:

RGB and CMYK Color Models

A graphic designer should know the difference between the RGB color model and CMYK color models, and which to use for the desired output. RGB is an additive color model that has richer colors and a broader color spectrum. It uses red, green, and blue primary colors at various intensities and uses light to superimpose the colors. The RGB color model is widely used in the design industry for projects that will primarily be for digital use.

The CMYK color model is known as the four-color process and is mostly used for printing purposes. It is a subtractive color process that uses inks to create the colors. Think paints, dyes, and inks. CMYK reduces the brightness or reflected light from the background of an image by working through the colors cyan, magenta, yellow, and true black (which is all three colors mixed) in order to achieve the desired color.

Understanding the difference between color models is important because this greatly affects the printing output of your cover design. The RGB color model is best for digital-only designs, while the CMYK color model is best for printing. Your graphic designer should understand how to convert from RGB to CMYK for printing.

Cut and Bleed Lines

If you are seeking a graphic designer, you'll want to hire one who knows how to prep files for printing. This includes setting up cut lines and bleed lines on your cover art file. Bleed lines are additional space beyond the book's trim size where the cover art must extend for your book to be printed with full bleed. If there are no bleeds set up on your cover art print files, your cover will print with white edging. Cut lines are also called trim marks and are essentially where the printer will trim the paper stock. The cut and bleed lines provide the printer with the information they need to properly print your cover design so that all important elements are within those specifications and no data is lost to the edges.

Image Resolution, Stock Licensing, and Image-Acaling

Licensing. The biggest part of the cover design is the visual component. A designer often uses licensed commercial stock images, elements, and graphics to create a custom cover design. If you hire someone who does not understand copyright licensing and stock usage policies, you risk landing in financial hot water from image copyright owners.

Most images online are not copyright-free or permitted to use. Regardless of whether a copyright symbol is visible on the image, it is best to assume it is copyrighted. Most images found on the internet are, because copyright is automatically applied to any publicly transmitted work.

There are dedicated sites that knowledgeable designers use to purchase licensed images for their art. This route keeps both the designer and the client safe from infringement.

Scaling. It is important to properly edit, resize, and/or manipulate graphics for your cover art without distortion or pixelation. Enlarging an image that's too small will cause it to lose vital details and look blurry. Details in design are important.

Image resolution. Designing for the proper output is crucial. Image resolution and color model often go hand in hand. Knowing which format and location your graphics will be published helps to determine the resolution and color model that will be needed.

Many printers require the color model CMYK and a minimum of 300 DPI (dots per inch) or 300 PPI (pixels per inch) for resolution output. The higher the resolution, the better the quality.

Ebooks and other digital-only publications are a bit more lenient. Often, the best resolution output is between 72-150 DPI.

BOOK GENRE

It is vital that your cover design is distinct and unique, but it also must align with the genre. Your preferred designer should be knowledgeable about your genre. Graphic designers specializing in book cover design often do research on their client's genre in order to determine the style which sells best, stands out, and would be best suited for their client's project.

A few questions you should ask when choosing your designer:

Are they familiar with your book's genre?
A designer who isn't familiar with your genre and isn't interested in researching it is likely not the ideal designer for your project.

What is their process for concept design development?
How does the designer find inspiration for their concepts? Where do they get their graphics? Do they illustrate the work themselves? Knowing details of how the designer works can help you determine if their style is what you're looking for.

Do they have a portfolio of past work?
Inquiring about previous work projects is important because you should be able to see the skill set and style a designer is offering through their portfolio.

What is their payment structure and fee for services?
Some designers require half payment upfront with the balance due upon completion, which is fairly standard for this trade.

Knowing your budget and timeline of payments is essential. It is also important to inquire about contracts to outline payments as well as details and scope of work.

Can they provide an estimated turnaround time?
As a designer, sometimes providing a turnaround time on a project is a bit difficult, but they should still be able to offer a rough idea of when the project will be completed.

How will the final product be delivered to you?
You need to know what you will be receiving and how the designer will be releasing the files to you.

What other design services do they offer?
Graphic designers often wear many hats. Book cover design is one of a plethora of wonderful and creative aspects of our job. As an example, in addition to book cover design, I also provide speaker sheets, business cards, bookmarks, event display design, and so much more. Authors I have worked with come back to me again for their marketing needs, and I am more than happy to help. Asking what other services your designer offers can save you time and energy in the event that you have other design or marketing needs in the future.

Can they provide past client references?
Having a designer who is able and willing to share testimonials, reviews, and even refer you directly to past clients for firsthand reference can help you determine the quality, customer service, and overall experience you'll receive working with them.

Every graphic designer operates a little bit differently. You could say we all have our own rhythm. But one thing that many of us all agree on is that we want to talk to you! A consultation is the best way to get to know you and learn about your book so we can find out if we're the right fit.

The initial consultation is also the perfect opportunity for you to get to know us and our process and get a feel for how well you and your designer could work together. Ask *all* the questions! Do not hesitate to ask about something you don't understand or request past client references.

Use this time to also find out how often you'll be given updates on your project. This can vary from designer to designer, but I often give updates multiple times a week via email. This way, I ensure that my clients know they are a priority to me and my business. My clients will walk away with quality work, gain knowledge from the experience, and maybe even make a new networking connection.

In my consultations, I explain my design process, educate my potential client on color psychology, and guide them on ways they can better visually represent their brand or story. I strive to connect with my clients and understand the message they want to convey with their visuals.

Over the past decade that I've spent working on various projects as a freelance graphic design artist, I've developed an eye for designing visuals that capture attention and help clients grow their business. But my journey to design has been unorthodox and came entirely by accident.

Life isn't about finding yourself; it's about creating yourself.
—Anonymous

I struggled with depression and severe anxiety due to family trauma, and I found myself fighting for a way—any way—out of the darkness. I was numb. I wanted to feel connected, to be helpful, and to bring joy again. So I began using digital art as my outlet. I placed my creations online via a print-on-demand platform and thought nothing of it... then people began to purchase them! I began receiving custom orders for wedding stationery, ministry slide decks, business cards, and so many other things. I was beside myself and completely astonished.

Feeling like others wanted to connect with me and were inviting me to be a part of their projects was so humbling and gave me a sense of purpose I had never experienced before. That's when I realized this was what I wanted to do. A blessing came from a dark cloud—proof that we don't always know where we're going until we have arrived.

I sometimes say that I did not choose graphic design; it chose me. We all had big dreams as children. I wanted to be a singer, and the world would be my stage. I never imagined I would become so enveloped in the art world from behind a computer. Yet here I am.

It's interesting how what we think we want in life is not always what we are called for. We tend to follow our passions, and mine led me to graphic design. Perhaps yours is guiding you to write a book. If it is, may it also guide you to the right graphic designer for your project.

Don't skimp on your cover art, because it tells your story too. Hire a graphic designer to help you connect your story with a powerful visual that will reach your target readers, capture their attention, and get your book in their hands.

ABOUT THE AUTHOR

After spending a decade working as a freelance contractor, Kristina Conatser has developed an eye for designing visuals that capture attention and help clients to grow their businesses. Her background in customer service means she also understands the importance of quality communication and customer satisfaction. With a passion for helping others and the drive to create an experience that is "people first," Kristina launched her own graphic design business, Captured by KC Designs, in 2022. Captured by KC Designs is a BBB-accredited graphic design and certified print reseller service that assists startups, small to medium-sized businesses, and entrepreneurs with the creative process in order to help them reach their target audience.

Kristina Conatser is a wearer of many hats and doer of many things. When she isn't lost in the world of Adobe programs, Kristina can be found in her home in North Carolina, wearing her supermom cape as an ever-ready, on-the-go mom of multiples.

Connect with Kristina:
- ➢ Website: capturedbykcdesigns.com
- ➢ Facebook: facebook.com/capturedbykcdesigns
- ➢ Instagram: instagram.com/captured_by_kc
- ➢ TikTok: tiktok.com/@capturedbykc
- ➢ LinkedIn: linkedin.com/in/capturedbykc

Chapter 14

How to Brand Your Book and Create a Legacy

by Meagan Caesar

Picture this… You've taken the huge leap and finally decided to write a book. Maybe you're sharing your story in a multiauthor collaboration. Maybe you're going solo. Maybe you're self-publishing or choosing one of the myriad other ways you can get your words out there. Or maybe you're a publisher supporting others to share the gift of their words. Whatever the scenario, you've chosen to share your voice, your message, with the world, and the words are flowing out.

Then it comes time to launch and you realise that writing a book is all well and good, but now you have to market it. Let's not go overboard and say the writing part was easy, but at least you understood the brief and knew what you had to do. Everything was focused on your zone of genius—speaking about what you love and what sets your soul on fire, and sharing your personal story. But now… now you realise you actually have to *sell* your book in order for it to become a bestseller. You have no idea where to start, or you're overwhelmed with all the things that go into a successful launch, and you just don't have the bandwidth to think about launch strategy or how to get your potential readers excited to buy your book.

I totally get it. I was you! And now I use that experience, along with my skills, to support authors and publishers throughout the publishing and marketing process. My work is an ever-evolving mélange of organisational skills, social media knowledge, editing, and visual creativity. I help authors and publishers build a consistent brand for their book, set up systems to support them during the book-writing and launch journey, provide editing and book cover design services, and create beautiful graphics and videos to connect their book with their aligned audience.

Ever since I was young, I've loved writing and dreamt of being an author. I've also always been incredibly organised. I love lists and systems that support me to save time, operate efficiently, and keep me on track. Take me to a stationery store and I'm in heaven! So many notepads, calendars, planners, diaries, just waiting to be filled! And don't even get me started on my excitement for all things in the digital organisation realm. But if you're anything like me, you may have struggled with getting caught up in the 'planning' and forgetting about the 'doing'. Often, for me, this was because I was overwhelmed with some of the tasks on my lists. I didn't know where to start, the learning curve to complete the task felt way too steep, or I didn't have a good system in place to help me get it done. Throw motherhood into the mix and my natural inclination for organisation was suddenly a non-negotiable; I had to let go of the procrastination and set up systems that actually supported me instead of adding to the overwhelm.

In my conventional life, I'm a high school English teacher. You can probably understand that organisation, systems, a desire to learn and share knowledge, and a love of words and stories are pretty essential to excelling in that role. It wasn't until I began my entrepreneurial journey with an affiliate marketing business at the start of 2020, after the birth of my second child, that I really began to shift my skill set towards helping others within the realm of online business, thereby discovering my talent for, and love of, graphic design. A connection within that community introduced me to a multiauthor book opportunity and I became an international bestselling author in mid-2021. This was the moment that catapulted me into the next exciting chapter (pun intended!) of my journey, because it introduced me to the publishing industry. And thanks to the support, belief, and advice of my incredible publisher (who is also sharing her story in this book), I branched out into creating social media reels and marketing graphics for book launches.

During this time, I was also transitioning to begin home-schooling my two children and setting up a beautiful, connected tribe of home-schooling mummas so we could support each other on this new and challenging voyage. It was this experience that allowed me to tap into and hone my natural organisational talents, and my gorgeous new village of mummas encouraged me to explore using those skills within my business to serve others.

If you're a person who's inherently organised, who likes to keep things tidy, is consistent with planning, and has systems in place to support you in your life and business, then it can be difficult to understand what it's like *not* to be like that. What I was discovering more and more through my work with publishers and authors, my affiliate business, and within our home-schooling group, is that many people struggle with those things. They feel foreign, overwhelming, hard to maintain. Throw in a digital learning curve and the struggle is real! Some people want to have these support structures in place but just don't know where to start, what tools to use, or how to set it all up. Or they lack the time to learn to do it all, because it doesn't come naturally. It. Just. Feels. Too. Hard. It's another thing on top of an already overfull to-do list, so it gets pushed to the side and they muddle through without a clear system, which inevitably leads to more stress and overwhelm.

At this point, you may be wondering, *What does any of this have to do with branding a book?*

Well, the realisation that so many people struggle with all of this was the light-bulb moment that really cemented my purpose, the way I can truly serve budding authors and busy publishers to feel confident, organised, and in control of their book launch. It's what sets me apart from others in my area of expertise. I don't just create your graphics and send you on your way. I have a range of options to support you in getting set up for success within your book launch and wider business. I offer simple systems, time-saving tips, education, and easy-to-follow strategies that eliminate that feeling of overwhelm, especially if the marketing side of bookselling isn't your forte.

I believe that organisation, consistency, education, and elements of automation are key in all aspects of business, especially to be able to grow and avoid burnout. This includes the business of writing and selling books. But they aren't everyone's cup of tea, so that's where I come in. You're writing a book because you want to share your story, your experience, with as many people as possible. You want to impact other people's lives with your words. But to do that… you need to *sell* your book! Writing a bestselling book isn't only about the 'writing'. It's not called a *bestselling* book for nothing! And to sell your book successfully, you need a plan and ways to minimise the overwhelm from the plethora of demands during the entire process.

Sales = Readers

Readers = Impact!

I think award-winning author, Erin Morgenstern, sums it up perfectly when she says, 'You may tell a tale that takes up residence in someone's soul, becomes their blood, and self, and purpose. That tale will move them and drive them, and who knows what they might do because of it, because of your words. That is your role, your gift'. Your story is your gift! A gift that you're bravely sharing with the world. A gift that you want to get into as many hands as possible. And you know what you need to do to make that happen? Yep, you guessed it! You need to market and sell your book, whether that's through news media, podcasts, social media, book-signings, or other forms of visibility. And that whole process can feel so incredibly daunting for a lot of people.

That's what I love about the concept of this book—you can find support and services to help you with every facet of the publishing journey. And it *is* a journey. If you've never written a book or a chapter for a multiauthor collaboration before, it's hard to grasp just how life-changing, healing, challenging, and eye-opening the process is. That's why you want to soak up the whole experience, leverage the support around you, go all-in, and do everything in your power to make your book a smashing success. And I'll be right there with you! One of my favourite parts of being involved in publishing books is the launch itself, getting to cheer the authors on, share their book with my audience, show others what's possible, and celebrate what an incredible milestone it is to write and publish your very own book.

I consider it a huge honour to play a small part in sharing your words with the world. As a teacher, I'm someone who naturally enjoys facilitating learning and providing support that fosters independence and empowers others to feel confident. So the merging of my organisational and teaching skills with my graphic design flair was an organic progression of my business. It's this unique blend of support systems, education, automation, and visual artistry that keeps my clients coming back. Some are looking for a starting point, a suite of templates to use however they need, a basic outline where the time-consuming setup has been done, and they can manage from there. Others are ready to leverage my zone of genius so they can focus on theirs. They have me create everything for them—ready-to-use systems, graphics, and schedules—so their time can be spent writing, connecting with their audience, and serving their clients, rather than muddling through tasks that take them twice the time they do me.

So, what does it mean to brand your book?

When it comes to creating a brand for your book, most people think about the graphics. They are one of the key pieces, of course, but what many don't realise is that the strategy *behind* the visuals is just as important. Branding encompasses your approach, intention, cohesion, message, and so much more. That's where branding and marketing differ.

Marketing a book means you're out there promoting, sharing, bringing awareness to it, and actively working to 'sell' it. That's an essential part of birthing a book. If you don't *sell* your book... no one will read it. Marketing is a key component in reaching as many people as possible. But book *branding*... that's a whole other level. This is the bit that gets me super excited! You can market without branding, but branding your book prior to marketing creates a much greater impact on your audience. It's all about consistency and cohesion. The more consistent your book branding and marketing, the more your potential readers see and connect with you and your writing, and the more they are primed to buy your book. They get to know you and understand how you can help them, and your message resonates with the right people.

A consistent brand for your book means you're marketing with intention. You have a strategy. Your visuals are cohesive. Your book is instantly recognisable to your audience, because each post is visually linked through your branding. Each branded piece of content compounds your message. Your audience is repeatedly exposed to your book's premise and wisdom, and they come to trust that your book will serve them. That's why branding your book is an essential component in your marketing strategy. Some social media 'gurus' are saying the popular marketing concept of 'know, like, and trust' is dead. I don't think that's true, or that it ever will be. Most people still prefer to purchase something they feel they know from someone they know, someone they feel they can trust, a person or product that's been recommended to them or that they've connected with on a level that allows them to feel understood, safe, and supported. It's no different when it comes to buying a book, especially ones within the nonfiction, spiritual, business, and personal development genres. Your book needs to stand out, be memorable, and speak with authority to your potential readers. Book branding allows it to do just that.

Choosing to write a book, or a chapter within a book collaboration, is no small thing. Whether you're sharing a personal story or writing as an authority within your industry, becoming a published author is an honour and an exciting milestone, and it can produce unexpected benefits if you commit to making the most of the experience. Book branding is one of the key ways you can do that, because branding your book means you're giving your words the very best chance to be seen, giving your book life, and creating a legacy to ensure your book and the wisdom you've shared within it never die.

Book branding is so much more than just pretty pictures or throwing up a few social media posts on launch day and hoping enough people will see them.

Book branding

- shares the soul of your writing with your potential readers,
- helps them understand how you and your book can help them,
- gives them a true sense of what your book is about and gets them excited to read it for themselves,

- builds credibility and authority,
- allows your audience to trust you because the consistency, quality, and value of what you share in the lead-up to launch shows them you are someone they can count on,
- makes consistent marketing possible, and consistent marketing primes your readers to purchase your book on launch day and beyond, which is essential in birthing a book that never dies and continues to create impact long after launch day.

So, how do you brand your book and maximise exposure during your launch? Here are my top tips:

- Take the time to get graphic templates set up. Doing this early means you won't be overwhelmed at launch time, and you can be consistent with your marketing throughout the entire journey because you already have easily adaptable templates ready to use. The cohesion and consistency build trust with your audience because everything is working together, rather than being disjointed and difficult to follow because you threw something together at the last minute.
- This also means setting up your Canva organisation (or whichever platform you're using) so everything's easy to find and use. This might include creating a folder for your book, renaming images, and/or saving them in folders to make them easy to find; keeping the same size graphics in a single design so you can quickly see all your marketing assets and you don't get all tangled up switching between multiple, separate designs; sharing key folders or designs with your team (if you have one); and ensuring the Brand section is up to date with your book brand so your team can easily support you in this process.

- Audit your socials! Give your profiles a once-over well before you start marketing your book to ensure they're up to date, professional, match your brand and vibe, and contain all the key info your audience needs to continue building their relationship with you and your book. This could entail a Facebook or Instagram Story highlight specifically for your book, which would include a branded cover; a mailing list link in your bio or website with a specific landing page for your book; and info in your profile bio that ties back to your book.

- Put thought into the mix of content you're sharing and get a basic plan in place for the lead-up to launch, not just launch day itself. Yes, you want to post about your book and launch, but you also need to show who you are and share value that will show your potential readers how you and your book can help them. Some ideas could be a carousel post with your top tips, an interview series with your co-authors or short Lives where you share your expertise, Reels sharing behind the scenes or showing your personality, or a series of interactive Stories to engage your audience. Use branded graphics and images that match your book brand and your audience will subconsciously connect these posts with your book, even if you don't explicitly state it.

- Repurpose content across platforms. For example, with minimal adjustments an Instagram Reel can be repurposed on Facebook, TikTok, YouTube Shorts, and Pinterest Idea Pins. Don't dismiss the power of things like Stories, especially as they promote a more casual and interactive connection with your audience. A mailing list specifically for your book is also a good idea; you can repurpose social media or blog posts into an email newsletter or series of emails, plus it's a handy tool for book updates and launch details. Ultimately, the more eyes on your content; the more exposure to the variety of your content; the more value you deliver; the more credibility you build with your audience—the higher the chance of that audience turning into buyers and readers.

- Consider what you can outsource, what systems you can implement to make things easy and minimise the energy drain, and what options are available to help take things off your plate. Writing, publishing, and launching a book is a big process. It's time-consuming, involves a lot of different tasks, and often throws up unexpected challenges and learning curves, so the more support you can access, the more enjoyable and less stressful the journey will be. 'A good system shortens the road to the goal', as author Orison Swett Marden says, so make sure you have solid systems and support in place from the beginning.

Now, those are only six tips, six steps to get you started on planning a successful launch. There is so much more I could add. Maybe that feels daunting. Maybe it feels unachievable with your already busy schedule. Maybe you're not so great with all the tech and marketing stuff, and you're not sure how to do your book justice. That's okay! That's why we're here. That's why we've written this book. If you've been toying with the idea of writing a book, but the publishing and marketing process seems a bit too overwhelming, the fact that you're reading *this* book is your sign to take the leap and just do it! In this book alone, you have access to experts who can support you in every area of the whole experience. There's nothing to stop you and it doesn't have to be stressful! So, what are you waiting for?

And when you take that leap, I'll be right there cheering you on!

ABOUT THE AUTHOR

Meagan Caesar is the founder of Meag E Caesar, a digital organisation wiz, editor, and visual branding and systems educator. She helps authors, publishers, and female entrepreneurs ditch the overwhelm and never-ending to-do lists by creating marketing graphics and strategies and setting up easy-to-use systems that support them to thrive, scale, and launch with ease. Meagan believes in the power of a well-structured system to shift us from floundering to flow so that we can shine in our zone of genius. Meagan is herself an international bestselling author, home-schooling mumma, and high school teacher turned online entrepreneur, so she knows a thing or two about the impact well-implemented organisation, or the lack of it, can make in both life and business. She is a passionate supporter of women doing life on their terms through the freedom of online business. Meagan lives in Toowoomba, Australia, with her husband and two children.

Connect with Meagan:
- ➤ Instagram: instagram.com/meag.e.caesar
- ➤ Facebook: facebook.com/meagcaesar
- ➤ LinkedIn: linkedin.com/in/meagancaesar
- ➤ Website: meagecaesar.com

Chapter 15

Your Book's Launch Isn't the End of Its Story

How to Set Up Your Book to Reach New Audiences after the Launch Is Over

by Carolyn Choate

When you know who your ideal reader is, then marketing your book is as simple as putting it in front of them.

—Carolyn Choate

Not so long ago, books had a similar shelf life to milk. It might take you a year to write the manuscript, a year to interest an agent, a year to shop it to publishers, a year to prep it to publish, and after those four years of effort, your book would have about six weeks to swim… or sink.

When I first started writing and publishing books in the 1990s, the internet was in its infancy. Google didn't even exist (and when it came along, I didn't think it would beat out Yahoo). There were no ebooks, there was no Kindle. Amazon was just beginning.

So, pre-internet, how were books marketed? With a big launch. For most of the history of publishing, if your book didn't sell off the bookstore shelves in the first six weeks, the bookstores were not going to order any more copies and your book would disappear.

Even worse, if you didn't sell out your first print run you might struggle to get your next book published at all.

We all got used to focusing our book marketing activity, energy, and budget on that first six weeks after publication. And even though the world has changed, many haven't yet realized the new strategies available.

Now, in some ways there's no such thing as a book launch. You can sell your book any time and there's no "shelf life." Yes, making a big splash in the beginning can get you momentum. It's how you break into bestseller categories and it gives your book a nice push. But in truth, you can launch your book again any time you want. And you can just leave it up for sale in online bookstores indefinitely, bringing people to the page with your marketing.

Book publishing has changed profoundly since the '90s, for everyone from the author to the publisher to the reader. There are so many more things you can do to promote your book now, and it's far less costly too.

Walt Whitman self-published his book and then went selling it door-to-door. Thank goodness we don't need to do that anymore!

I published my first book on Amazon in 2009. The ability to set up a print-on-demand paperback was world-changing. You no longer needed to put all the investment in upfront or store mountains of books in your garage. Instead of printing books and then selling them, print-on-demand means that the book is only printed when someone buys one. And you don't have to pay to put the book up for sale; Amazon will take a cut from the purchase cost and pay you the rest.

It was revolutionary for the book world in multiple ways. It took away the gatekeepers.

People have mixed feelings about that. Having gatekeepers could be a good thing to keep the quality of books high, but now the gatekeepers are the readers. If you self-publish a book that isn't up to readers' expectations, they'll let you know and sales will be slow. (And I think we've all experienced traditionally published books that were terrible too!)

Let me tell you from personal experience, true validation comes not from a publisher accepting your manuscript, but from readers reacting to your work. It's the most incredible feeling in the world to have someone tell you that your book changed their life.

I had someone tell me that she gave my first book to her therapist because it explained how she was feeling better than she had been able to express. That was a book that publishers rejected because they couldn't see how they were going to market and position it. Yet, with the internet, that book found its people, and 13 years later, it still sells (with almost no active promotion).

Then something called ebooks started making waves.

When Amazon came out with the Kindle, I didn't take it seriously. (Are you seeing a theme? I'm not quick to adopt new things!) A friend suggested I put my book on Kindle and I said, "There's an ebook version on the vanity press website I used. If people really want it, it's there." (Now you don't even need to have one of these sites help you, as Amazon has their own service.) What I actually had in 2009 was a PDF that could be downloaded from a random site that no one had heard of.

When I finally tested out creating a version for Kindle, everything changed.

Buying ebooks is such a low cost of entry. People can try out a book for $5 and if they don't like it, it's not a huge loss. But if they do, they have found a new indie favorite.

There was a lot of argument back then about the pricing of ebooks. Regular publishers were charging the same price as a paperback and the market wasn't supporting that. To readers, the impression was that it costs less to produce an electronic book than a print book, so the price should be lower.

But how low? Writers had still put their blood, sweat, and tears into creating the story, and they deserved to be paid. Plus, many indie authors foot the bill for cover designers and editors. Yet, when the book price is lower, you could probably expect to sell a larger number of them. It's a balance.

It was an interesting time watching the fluctuations and changes. One of the first authors to put her work on Kindle became a millionaire on 99-cent ebooks. That doesn't happen anymore. The landscape is crowded now and you need to work harder to get your book found.

The good news is, that's in your control.

ALWAYS BE FUNNELING

I was creating sales funnels long before I knew what they were. Truth be told, there's nothing new about funnels, though they weren't always called that. It's simply a way of guiding someone on a journey towards your products and services. In other words, a codified client journey.

A funnel is like a marble run machine that you set up (usually on your own website), then you focus your marketing attention on the first step so you're bringing lots of marbles (people) to the starting point. Then the machine takes care of teaching them about your products and making offers to them. You can set up your marketing to guide people anywhere you want, including to an Amazon page that sells your book.

I joke that my personal hashtag is #AlwaysBeFunneling, but it's not entirely a joke. In everything I do online, I think about what the next step is and how I am guiding people there.

So, naturally, your book manuscript should also be funneling. When someone finishes reading your book, whether electronic or paper, do you offer them a next step?

For example, traditional publishers have long included teasers from the author's next book at the end of the current one. You can make it easy for readers to take that next step with a QR code in a print book or a link in an ebook.

While you can promote your Amazon book listing directly, it's far better to have a funnel on your own website where you offer visitors a lead magnet, or "reader magnet," for the internet currency of an email address and permission to contact them. That way you are able to personally connect with your readers and grow a powerful author platform.

Offer a chapter from your book or a short story in the same theme for free. Once they request the reader magnet, you deliver it to their email address and then keep in touch with them, sharing behind the scenes of your business and your writing, fun memes you see, quotes that inspire you, and resources your ideal readers will find useful. And then when you have something to promote, you've got an audience eager and ready to hear about it!

Some people build their author platform on a social platform. While growing an online audience is great, it's important to focus on funneling those people back to your reader magnet and onto your email list. A social platform can kick you out at any moment. It could go out of business, your account could be hacked, you could go to social jail... and then you can't communicate with your audience. Your email list is yours, that no one can take from you.

So, now you have a "top-of-funnel" link to promote, whether that's to your free reader magnet or your book's Amazon page, and you have to get new people to see it.

That's called bringing traffic to your funnel. There are four types of website traffic and lots of methods within each that you can try until you find a good combination for you and your audience.

As a marketer, I must give you the caveat that there is no magic tactic, no one right way to market your book that will ensure everything will be smooth. A lot of marketers out there will try to tell you that they have some secret formula that works better than all the others, and if you pay them, they will show you how to do it.

I like to get paid as much as the next gal, but what I have discovered in the course of my work is that the marketing tactic that works is the one that is aligned to your heart. And no AI copywriting will ever beat the words that come directly from your heart and soul.

The exact funnel and formula that made one person $3 million dollars in a year will be a total dud for another person. The difference is what aligns with your values and beliefs, and how you connect with your audience. (I learned this the hard way, spending money I didn't have to learn ClickFunnels and a style of marketing that makes me uncomfortable. Even as I followed every instruction and every script, it didn't work for me at all.)

So, with that out of the way, let me tell you some of the ways you can bring people to your funnel or your book page so you can continue to reach new people forever.

FOUR PILLARS OF TRAFFIC

- Inbound organic
- Outbound organic
- Borrowed
- Paid

Inbound organic is my personal comfort zone. Organic means that you haven't paid to get in front of people; it's not social media ads or a sponsorship. Inbound means that you are drawing people to you with the content you put out.

This includes posting on LinkedIn or TikTok. It also includes writing a blog. It is pinning on Pinterest. It is SEO, which stands for search engine optimization.

While the topic of SEO could fill a whole book by itself, here's the simple version: Think about your ideal reader and what problem they want to solve that has them heading to Google to search. Whatever problem it is, it's something that you or your book solves. So, what words are they typing into the search bar looking for the solution that you offer? (And remember, that problem can be as simple as they're bored and want to escape with a novel.)

Take the words and phrases that they are probably putting into search engines and use them in your posts, on your website, in your book description, on your Amazon page, in pin descriptions, and especially in blog posts. (By the way, every blog post should include a call to action that invites the reader to the next step of the funnel, such as "Download this chapter to learn xyz." #AlwaysBeFunneling)

Outbound organic is Walt Whitman knocking on people's doors. It's cold messaging, reaching out to people who don't know you to offer them something. (In full transparency, this is my least favorite traffic method and I very rarely use it, but it can have its place.)

Borrowed traffic is really cool. This is where you leverage your network and relationships to get introduced to new audiences. When you get invited to speak on someone's podcast about your book's topic, then you get a warm introduction to that person's entire audience. You can take yourself on a whole podcast book tour! Ten years ago, blog tours were very in; these days podcast tours are preferred. By the time you're reading this, there might be another popular way of getting in front of other people's audiences, but the principles are the same: Where are your ideal readers hanging out? Who out there already has their attention? Talk to that person!

Finally, paid traffic is ads such as Facebook ads, Amazon ads, promoted pins, boosted posts, or putting an ad on a forum where your ideal readers hang out.

Once you have a humming funnel, adding paid traffic will bring your little campfire to a bonfire. However, I always recommend people start with getting organic sales before adding in paid traffic, because you can end up spending a lot of money very quickly trying to get them working.

Sometimes it's the ad itself that needs testing and optimizing, but sometimes you're paying to bring people to a bad funnel that isn't going to get anyone to buy or join your email list. Once you've made some sales from organic methods, then you know your funnel is working and you can start increasing the number of people you bring over with paid ads.

They sky's the limit, so get creative with how you promote your book. Even if you self-publish, you can still get into bookstores, have a launch party (I know someone who does amazing virtual book launch parties), and sign books for your fans. One author I interviewed on my podcast signs bookplate stickers that he mails to fans to attach to the books they've bought so he doesn't have to buy and ship out hard copies.

No matter how you promote your book, remember the most important first step: knowing who is most going to want to read your book and speaking to that person. The more specific and clear you can be, the more rabid your fans will be!

The book that publishers and agents rejected because they couldn't figure out how to market it has a dedicated fan base because I knew who the perfect readers for it were and how to reach them.

There's now no limit to how many people you can reach with your book.

ABOUT THE AUTHOR

Carolyn Choate is the founder of Financially Free Author. She is known as the heart-guided sales funnel-builder. She helps coaches, speakers, and authors leverage their books *after* the launch to grow and scale their business.

She is the host of *The Financially Free Author Show*, has written books in a variety of genres, and was publishing during the wild west of ebook publishing when Kindle first came out. She loves all things marketing-tech and systems.

Carolyn enjoys surprising people on Zoom with her knee-length hair and playing board games with her husband.

Learn all about her Funnel Mapping Strategy Sessions at:

➤ financiallyfreeauthor.com

Connect with Carolyn:

➤ Instagram: instagram.com/financiallyfreeauthors
➤ YouTube: youtube.com/@financiallyfreeauthor
➤ financiallyfreeauthor.com

Chapter 16

You Are Your No. 1 Spokesperson

Time to Launch Your Book

by Nicolette Halladay

So you're ready to launch your book. As I mentioned in the Introduction, only 3 percent of people who start writing a book actually finish it. You made it to the 3 Percent Club—that in itself is a major achievement. Welcome to the club, and congratulations!

You did the hard work of writing and polishing your manuscript, and now you're preparing to share your book with the world. Whether you decide to go the traditional publishing route, self-publish, or use a hybrid publisher, it will be up to you to make sure that as many people as possible know about your book. Whatever you do, now is not the time to hold back. You are the number one spokesperson for your book, and in order to get it in people's hands, you have to be willing to shout it from the rooftops. You did something amazing… You wrote a book! You have an important message or a compelling story to share, and now it's time to send it out into the world with the love and gusto it deserves.

But how do you do that, exactly? There are numerous resources available on self-publishing and book promotion—everything from uploading your book on Kindle Direct Publishing, to strategically selecting the best keywords and categories to leverage Amazon's algorithms for a bestselling campaign, and utilizing platforms like IngramSpark for larger distribution channels. But what you're not likely to find is information about managing your mindset and energetics during a book launch. As a publisher, I can attest that this is arguably one of the most important aspects.

How can you promote your book and sell as many copies as possible naturally and organically, while also having the time of your life? That's what we're going to explore in this chapter, with some tangible steps to help you get there. But first, let's discuss a few of the roadblocks you'll need to be aware of so you can gracefully navigate around them and stay focused on the prize.

Having helped bring over 20 books to market in the last couple years, I can definitively say that right before you launch your book is when imposter syndrome, feelings of unworthiness, and perfectionism can kick in. Some of the most confident authors crumble when it's time to share their project with the world. I've seen debilitating beliefs derail and even stop book launches in their tracks.

Who am I to share this story?

Who am I to publish a book?

What might people think of me?

You might be surprised at the number of completely finished books that don't make it to the market because the author falls victim to self-sabotage right when it's time to own their confidence and promote their book.

It can be scary to put yourself out there in a new way, and it's normal to feel uncomfortable about how that new version of you might be perceived, especially when it's center stage for the whole world, including your friends and family, to see. But books aren't sold when authors aren't comfortable talking about their work, and the more you share about it, the more people will have the opportunity to read it and be impacted by it.

So, when embarking on a creative endeavor or doing something that is going to push us outside our comfort zone, it's important to manage our energy. And luckily, one of the most crucial things we can do to ensure a successful outcome is prioritize self-care. Just as important as doing tangible work like maintaining a consistent writing practice or preparing our launch team, doing things that make us feel nurtured, inspired, and taken care of is equally important.

The cool thing about prioritizing self-care is that when you feel good, you work well. Writing that would normally take hours is accomplished in half the time and is more eloquently expressed. All of a sudden, you're clearer, more efficient, and more dynamic.

It can be difficult to be creative and productive when we don't feel inspired. Even though there will be times that we have to work when we don't feel like it, the idea that we need to grind through day after uninspired day is counterproductive. It's doubtful that every minute you spend working on your book will be blissful, which is all the more reason to prioritize doing the things that make you feel good.

Here are five things you can do to make the book promotion process more enjoyable, inspiring, and ultimately successful.

Make a Light Infusion List

I encourage my clients to make a "light infusion list," or a list of things they enjoy doing. For me, this list includes meditating, spending time in nature, open-water swimming, exercising, spending time with friends and family, taking long baths, writing in my journal, coloring, reading, and visiting nearby hot springs. I expect your list to be as unique as you are and filled with things that can be done in just a few minutes, like 10 deep breaths, or things you can get caught up doing for hours. Making sure your list includes both easily accessible items that don't require a lot of time or resources as well as grander indulgences will ensure you always have things you can do to tap into those feel-good vibes.

When things get busy, it's easy to neglect doing the things that make us most happy. What if I told you that how you feel has a direct impact on the success of your book? Would you prioritize doing the things you love? Contrary to popular opinion, grueling hours and sacrificing our happiness are counterproductive to successfully bringing a book into the world.

Nourish Your Body

Take care of yourself by nourishing your body while you're promoting your book. Drink plenty of water, eat nourishing foods, get consistent exercise, and stay well rested—these are the bedrock of physical well-being. It's not going to be good enough to eat junk food and sit on the couch stressing about how this book is going to be received. Nourishing your body is the foundation for how you feel, and being intentional about that is going to set the framework for everything else. This might not be the time for a complete health overhaul, but a few tweaks to your existing routine can have a big impact.

Create Your Support Team

Surround yourself with people who are going to support you. These won't always be the ones in your immediate circle. Expecting those people to be your support team if they don't genuinely want to be can cause friction and hurt feelings that can wreck your self-esteem precisely when you need to shine. It's important to recognize this early and find the people who will cheer you on. These are the same people who might also be a part of your launch team later. Whether they see your vision and want to help you share it with the world or are simply proud of you and want to see you succeed, their support can help keep you buoyant and encouraged.

Visualize Your Success

Visualize your success and the impact your book will have every day. Hold that vision in your mind's eye and get excited thinking about it. See the success of your book as it makes its debut in the world. See yourself talking about the book, being interviewed, and attending book-signings and launch parties. Imagine this book being lovingly received and cherished by readers. Anchoring in the long-term benefits of this book for your life and career will help you keep your book launch moving forward rather than allow things to derail due to a temporary setback or disappointment. Feel pride in what you have accomplished and know that great things are coming your way because of your efforts.

Keep in Mind the People You Want to Reach and the Impact This Book Will Have on Their Lives

Whether your book is here to provide entertainment, education, wisdom, or perspective, the reason you wrote it is so other people could have a chance to receive the message you came to share. Most often, when people are affected by imposter syndrome, it's because they're making their book too much about themselves and not enough about the people they're here to serve. But in the end, this really isn't even about you, is it? Remembering the impact this book will have on your readers' and potential clients' lives shifts the focus from you to your audience.

Yes, you accomplished a wonderful thing by publishing your book, but now give the book a chance to be bigger than you. Switching the focus to your audience will also help with putting yourself out there in new and possibly uncomfortable ways, because you'll be more likely to "be scared and do it anyway" when you think about the people all this effort will ultimately serve.

Now that you've created a supportive environment for yourself and you're feeling confident about sharing your book with the world, let's talk about the concrete steps you can take to get your book out there and garner additional exposure and attention, both during the initial launch and as a long-term strategy for selling more copies of your book.

While it's true that you are the biggest spokesperson for your book, assembling a launch team and enlisting the help of others can mean the difference between selling a handful of copies or hundreds or even thousands of copies. Let's talk about some ways we can get others on board for your launch.

Having book launch support means that instead of being the only one sharing, talking about, and promoting your book, you have other people supporting you in your efforts. Not only does it expand the reach of your book, it also makes the book launch less lonely and more fun.

There are multiple levels of support people can offer during a book launch and many ways their assistance can be structured:

ENLISTING YOUR AUDIENCE

Your audience and top fans are eagerly anticipating the release of your book, so enlisting their support makes a lot of sense for a few different reasons. It guides them on how they can purchase the book, leave an early review, and share it with people they believe will also benefit. It helps them feel like they are part of the launch, which many of your top fans will go crazy for. Plus, just by reaching out to your audience beforehand and letting them know about the different ways to support you during the launch, you'll drive more sales on day one.

Here's a simple template on how you can engage your audience:

I'm looking for [number of people based on your audience size] to support my book launch by purchasing [name of book] for just [price] when it is released on [date].

Here are three ways you can support us:

1. *Purchase a copy when the book is released.*
2. *Purchase a copy when the book is released and leave an early 5-star review.*
3. *Purchase a copy when the book is released, leave an early 5-star review, and share it with your social media audience or directly with people you think would like to purchase the book.*

Let us know how we can count on your support.

BUILD YOUR LAUNCH TEAM

A launch team is a group of people that come together to build excitement about your book and help with the actual launch. You are, in essence, borrowing other people's platforms for a short period in order to give your book the widest reach possible.

Depending on your book, your existing audience, and where you are in your author or business journey, there's a good chance you already know who these people are—friends, family, colleagues, mentors, clients, employees, or raving fans. People who want to see your book launch succeed may want to see behind the scenes of a launch or get early access, bonuses, or closer access to you as the author—all things you can offer in exchange for their support.

Enlist help with promotion, public relations (PR), networking, and expanding your reach with the book. You'd be surprised at how many people would love to help if you only give them the opportunity.

MAKING THE MOST OUT OF YOUR BOOK

I've seen authors who contribute to a multiauthor book tap into every possible avenue of growth the book has available to them and continue to use it in their marketing even a year after it's published. And I've seen people who do nothing more than share about it during the launch and then never utilize it again. Guess who gets more recognition, leverage, exposure, and clients?

Ultimately, you are responsible for your own experience, and how big of an impact you want to make is up to you. I'm here to provide you with fun and exciting ways you can keep sharing about your book. If you take advantage of each of these, I promise your book is going to have a bigger impact.

- Add book links to your website, or better yet, create a book page on your website with links to purchase the book, a synopsis of the book, and pictures of you with your book, along with what topics you love to speak about, interviews you've had, and media attention you've received from your book.
- Create a one-sheet for pitching to podcasts and other media outlets that might be interested in interviewing you. Include details about your book, who you're hoping to reach, and the impact you want to have, and start pitching to aligned outlets.
- Plan a local or virtual workshop where you can read excerpts from your book, promote your offerings, and start building a local community. It's crazy how many people don't tap into their local community when it comes to promoting their book and associated services.
- Contact organizations with a similar mission and tell them about your book to see if there is a chance for collaboration or cross-promotion.
- Give people a chapter in your book as an opt-in or freebie on your website in exchange for their

email address. This is a great way to encourage book purchases as well as collect email addresses for future direct promotion.

- Give away copies of the book in a contest. This draws on two things people love: winning and free stuff! Drive interest and excitement by creating a contest within your audience where people have a chance at winning a free and perhaps signed copy of the book.
- Reach out to local bookstores and see if they'd be interested in selling your books. You can coordinate this with a book-signing and local PR campaign to get additional exposure for your book and the bookstore that's hosting it.
- Organize a book-signing at a local yoga studio, coffee shop, bookstore, or chamber of commerce. Combine this with a local PR campaign to get additional exposure for your book and the organization hosting the event.
- Use your book as a networking tool. Send a copy of your book with a handwritten letter to people you would love to network and partner with.
- Host a booth at a local farmer's market, fair, or festival with copies of your book and opportunities to work with you.

Feeling good, enlisting support, and leveraging creative ways to share your book with more people aren't just going to add to the success of your book, they will create a more enjoyable publishing experience. I want you to see this as an opportunity to grow professionally and personally while having the time of your life. Publishing and promoting your book can feel like you're dredging through mud that you're in a hurry to get through, or it can feel like you're having a party and inviting everyone else to celebrate with you. You get to decide.

If I get a vote, then I say, "Let's have a party!" You published your book! It's time to celebrate.

ABOUT THE AUTHOR

Making waves in the publishing world, bestselling author Nicolette Halladay is the CEO of Inspired Hearts Publishing. A storyteller, a publisher, and a purpose-seeker, she is here to help entrepreneurs, creatives, and changemakers find the courage to be seen and heard.

After spending five years behind the scenes supporting other businesses as a virtual assistant, she decided it was time to stop hiding. She felt called to help women who had stories just like her take center stage by becoming published authors.

She's on a mission to create a world where aspiring leaders can become published authors without gatekeepers—using the pen to empower and amplify women's voices one book at a time!

Embracing life's adventures with her three wild and wonderful daughters, this Colorado native is a lover of all things outdoors and is passionate about connecting with others.

Follow her journey to inspire, empower, and equip the next generation of thought leaders!

Connect with Nicolette:

- ➤ Website: inspiredheartspublishing.com
- ➤ Facebook: facebook.com/nikki.richardsonhalladay
- ➤ Instagram: instagram.com/nicolettehalladay111
- ➤ LinkedIn: linkedin.com/in/nikki-halladay

Chapter 17

The Art of Being Seen

by Bridget Sicsko

Understand this if you understand nothing: It is a powerful thing to be seen.

—Akwaeke Emezi

Writing a book is such an act of service, not only for your future readers and fans, but for you as the author. You are giving yourself the gift of being loved, seen, heard, and understood, which, to me (and numerous research studies), are some of our most basic human needs, beyond safety, food, security, protection, and water, of course.

Now, you might be thinking, *What does any of that have to do with visibility and the promotion of my book?*

You see, the art of being seen actually comes with some weight. The weight of…

How do I get this book out there to as many people as possible?

What strategies do I implement to reach my audience?

What does this book represent, and what is my message?

How do I hold steady and not waver with more eyes and ears on my brand?

How do I navigate the pressure of visibility and being seen?

I believe visibility is a nuanced topic that means different things to different people, so in this chapter, I'm going to guide you through both the tangible and intangible steps to help you shine as an emerging author and brand figure.

By the way, I'm Bridget Aileen Sicsko. Over the last seven years, I've impacted thousands of leaders, founders, and entrepreneurs all over the world through my publishing company, podcast, speaking, and TV interviews. My mission is to help successful founders with a spiritual backbone stand out and be featured as leaders in their industry by sharing powerful stories, becoming a more poised and confident speaker, and gaining global recognition through podcasts, media features, and speaking. Truly, I believe in the power of words, stories, and voices to shift our view of reality, our potential, and our purpose on the planet.

I have always had a love of speaking, sharing, and connecting with people through words. In my own career, I've naturally found myself in this space of speaking and visibility; not through a college degree or education, but simply through experience. I was interviewed on my first podcast in 2017 and I've personally interviewed over 400 people over the last six years. I've spoken on stages, been on amazing podcasts, been published, and I'm even going to London this year to speak. I say all of that to say, I've done the tangibles, and I found that what is usually missing in your standard "brand yourself" or "be visible" training is *the unspoken art of being seen.* It's one thing to have the goal to show up. It's a whole other animal to take care of your inner landscape as the outer world asks more of you. Long story short, on a deeper level, I understand the energetics of visibility.

So you've written your book. Now what?

Allow me to introduce you to the *tangibles* of being seen as an emerging author: your message, your "it" factor, visibility avenues, and cross-promotional strategies.

YOUR MESSAGE

With a book, you've probably spent *a lot* of time getting clear on your message. You've probably had numerous rewrites to solidify that core message so that your reader knows exactly what they are getting out of your book. That same clarity is required for visibility.

For example, let's say you run a real estate business and you just recently published your book, *How to Purchase Your First Home When You're Self-Employed.* Think of this from a consumer standpoint. Say someone lands on your website, your socials, your LinkedIn, or sees your book. Immediately, we need to make it crystal clear to this potential consumer what it is that you do. They should, without a shred of doubt, understand that you are the gal who runs the real estate business and shares content, information, and emails on topics like how to purchase your first home when you're self-employed.

I like to think of this message as a *mental imprint*. What is the mental imprint you are projecting with your book, socials, and public-facing presence? Clean up your website, socials, and Amazon book page if things aren't on point.

Pro tip: Ask a friend to tell you what they perceive your message to be from your content, emails, socials, and book. That's a great way to understand what the public is perceiving your mental imprint to be.

When it comes to visibility, we want the message to be clearly communicated. And since you've already written an entire book, you can take that message and broadcast it on your socials.

YOUR "IT" FACTOR

Think of this as your standout sparkle—what makes you unique from other people doing similar things.

As you emerge as a more visible author and brand figure, it's important to begin thinking about what sets you apart from the rest. I always love the reminder that our stories, experiences, and personal journeys are what set us apart from others even if we have a very similar message to someone else.

For instance, I am in a community with many fellow women publishers. Some could see that and say, "That's your competition. How are you going to beat them out?" My philosophy is a radically different road. Instead of "beating" them out, I get to ask myself, *What is my message? What do I do differently? How did I get here?*

At the end of the day, there are always different strokes for different folks, and what a blessing. With those questions, I'm able to understand that my main message is different and my backstory of healing, illness, and the voice is different from my fellow publishing friends.

So, I invite you to start thinking about your "it" factor. Let's say you wrote a book on the magic of a morning ritual. Ask yourself these questions:

- What is my message?
- What do I do differently?

- How did I get here?
- What is my story?
- How does my message differ from those around me?
- What makes my work unique?

From there, you can begin to lean into your unique message, knowing that your story will always set you apart from those around you, even if there are thousands of other people also speaking about morning rituals.

VISIBILITY AVENUES

Think of these as the many channels through which you could concretely disseminate a message.

For this section, I'm going to focus on some of my favorite and most easily accessible visibility avenues.

Social Media. I know it seems simple, but some authors never establish a social presence. And let's face it: It's 2023. Everyone's on socials. Like it or loathe it, some degree of presence is crucial. Instagram is a great platform to get started. Be sure to include a photo of yourself, a bit about you, and links to your book, website, events, and any other press related to your book. Use hashtags, go live with other authors (or brands with large audiences), and utilize cross-promotional strategies to build your audience.

Podcasts. According to Edison Research, 177 million people listened to podcasts in 2022. That is 177 million people to get in front of to share your message. The best part about podcasts is that they are so targeted. For instance, if I'm in the wellness space, I am usually going to listen to podcasts that talk about health, spirituality, and living my life's purpose. Therefore, I'd expect guests who can speak on those topics. And since podcasts are long-form storytelling content (which build the "know, like, and trust" factor), I am more likely to buy after listening to someone on a podcast. So, as the brand figure and author, you have the ability to get in front of your ideal audience who is buying.

Truelist.com has said that over 50 percent of listeners have made purchases after listening to a podcast. I am personally part of that number. Why did I choose to buy after listening to someone on a podcast? Honestly, it wasn't so much about what they taught. It was about the human connection I felt to them. In this day and age, we are moving to a relationship economy, meaning more and more people want to buy from—you guessed it—real people with real stories. From astrology readings to books, to hiring my mentor and buying my favorite products, *podcasts sell.*

So, how can you get yourself on a podcast? Once you have your main message or a number of solid topics to speak about, I recommend you introduce yourself to podcast hosts. There are numerous free Facebook communities looking for podcast guests which are great for newer guests and speakers. If you'd like to get on larger shows, I recommend doing some research, starting with mid-tier shows. Google the show, the ideal audience, and who the host is. After you have that information, you can write an email pitch introducing yourself. Be sure to include information about your brand, what makes you stand out, accolades, past interviews, and contact information.

Media (digital and print publications, stages, TV, radio). Beyond podcasts, you also have the ability to land amazing media features that can be broadcast in front of millions. Most authors and brands see media giants like major news stations (Fox, ABC, CNN) and large publications (*Forbes, Business Insider, mindbodygreen*) as untouchable. But the truth of it is, anyone can introduce themselves to the media—authors, brands, and smaller business owners too.

Your next question is likely, "But how?"

You can represent yourself, and it all starts with nailing down your message, being positioned correctly, owning your "it" factor, knowing the topics you could easily comment or speak on, and understanding how the media works.

The media is an interesting beast. Editors, journalists, reporters, producers, and podcast hosts are looking for the best experts to help support their stories. For example, say a writer is doing a story on the real estate market in 2023, and you just wrote a book on the real estate market, so could easily speak on this. You introduce yourself to this writer and provide expert commentary on the topic. Ta-da! It's a win-win! For the sake of this chapter not being a gazillion pages long, I'll leave it at that, but here are some simple steps to begin approaching the media:

- Nail down your message, brand summary (a simple statement describing what it is that you do), brand story (how you got here), and your "it" factor (what differentiates you from others).
- Research media outlets (local news, radio, TV, aligned podcasts, digital and print publications).
- Create your pitch (your introduction to the media).
- Leverage past press *and* your book in your pitch.

Remember, it is possible for you to be featured on outlets like *Forbes* that reach over 140 million people worldwide.

CROSS-PROMOTIONAL STRATEGIES

Think of these as linking arms with people who are willing to support and uplift your message.

All of the above visibility avenues lend themselves nicely to being cross-promotional strategies. As someone who desires more visibility, you'll want to think about a simple concept: *getting in front of other people's audiences.*

When I was focused solely on growing my publishing company, I linked arms with as many people as I could—past clients, people who had a similar mission (but didn't offer publishing services), and people I met in networking spaces. I was solid on my message, I knew exactly who my ideal client was, I had concrete pricing, and I had a clear ask.

I wanted to be power partners or affiliate partners with them. When they shared my services with an ideal client and that client converted, they received a predetermined percentage of the total product price. This type of strategy helped me expand the publishing company and generate over $100,000 in revenue the first year in business, not to mention I built a lot of awesome relationships!

Youtubers do cross-promotion extremely well. They will bring their friends on their videos with them and make sure to mention each other's channels throughout the video. This leads to an uptick in traffic on both accounts.

Podcasts are another great example of cross-promotional strategy, because not only are you getting to share your message on someone's show, you are also going to share this episode with your audience. It's another win-win!

With your book, ask yourself, "Who can I link arms with to get my book into the hands of as many people as possible?"

Try this:

As an author, think of 10-20 people, visibility avenues, networks, or communities who would love to support not only your book, but your brand as you expand. We will call them your visibility partners. Below, I've listed some simple strategies to leverage a cross-promotional visibility campaign.

- Prepare an email for your visibility partners and have them email their list about your book launch.
- Reach out to a local business who would love to host your book launch event. You bring people to their store and you both get to tell people about your book/event.
- Have a program or product to offer that connects with the message in your book? Link arms with brands who

have a similar audience but don't offer exactly what you do. This becomes a value-add for both of you!

Now let's talk about what no one wants to talk about: *the intangibles.*

Being seen and having eyes on your business, your brand, your story, and what you do is no simple feat. It might seem like it's just about getting out there, utilizing the strategy, and reaping the rewards. But if you've picked up this book, chances are you are keen to understand the deeper work that's at play.

Throughout my career, I've worked with many business owners who know in their heart they have something of magnitude to share. They've seen themselves on stages in their meditations and have known for quite some time that they want to speak more and be seen as an authority. But something tends to stop them from pursuing these visibility avenues.

What is it?

Fear. Feeling not good enough. Unworthy of "that type" of attention. They want to run away and hide under a blanket.

So, how do you navigate these deep fears?

This is where my background in yoga, spiritual law, and the metaphysical come into play. Energetically, when the world asks more of you and there is more pressure on you, how do you, as I say, hold steady?

BEING PREPARED FOR YOUR SUCCESS

Since I was in high school, I've had a yoga practice. I came to the practice for not only the physical benefits (yes, I started with hot yoga to burn calories), but for the philosophy, mantras, and more. Because of my deep curiosity of the esoteric, I found myself drawn to kundalini yoga. And for the past seven years, I've been practicing and teaching kundalini yoga, the yoga of awareness. In kundalini yoga, there are many teachings on success, immunity, vitality, and the physical body. I've come to understand that when we expand and grow, we need our nervous system and physical body to be able to hold those new patterns.

My teacher used to relate this to lottery winners or child celebrities. They would have a lot of success at once, then lose it all. Why? They weren't prepared for their success.

So, as you emerge on the author stage and as an authority figure, let yourself dream of your success.

- What does your life look like?
- How do you spend your time?
- What needs to change for you to hold more success?
- How do you spend your money?

FEELING SAFE TO BE SEEN

This is another big topic in the visibility space, one that I believe needs to be navigated through the physical body with somatic practices, breathwork, as well as the subconscious mind through meditation, hypnosis, etc. Many of us carry the trauma and baggage from not only generations prior but also society at large. As a collective, there is a belief that it's not safe to be seen.

As you emerge on your visibility journey, begin to take a look at some of your beliefs around visibility and, if it's right for you, make time for practices that can support your nervous system as you expand. And it really helps to have a community behind you as you emerge. Find your people!

SHINE BRIGHTLY

You now have the tangible and intangible tools to move forward as an author. Remember that there is a reason you had the idea to share your story, wisdom, knowledge, and expertise in a book. It might have been just for you, but as one of my mentors always said, "What if there is someone out there praying for the message and work you do?"

Get out there and be seen for your fabulous work! Someone out there might just be kneeling, hands at their heart, looking for your message.

And of course, your message will always come at the right time, in the right way.

And so it is.

Shine brightly!

ABOUT THE AUTHOR

Bridget Aileen Sicsko is the founder of Exalted Publishing House and co-founder of her brainchild, Visibility on Purpose. She helps successful founders with a spiritual backbone stand out and be featured as leaders in their industry by sharing powerful stories, writing bestselling books, and gaining global recognition through speaking, podcasts, and media exposure. Beyond her business ventures, Bridget speaks on stages, hosts a top-rated podcast called *She Builds Empires*, and is an avid spiritual student and teacher. Ultimately, Bridget believes in the power of words, stories, and voices to shift our view of reality, our potential, and our purpose on the planet. Bridget has appeared on *This Is It TV, Good Morning Arizona, Ticker News, RVN TV,* and *News 12 New York*; been featured in *AskMen, Formidable Woman Magazine, Authority Magazine, Women's Business Daily, Thrive Global,* and *Medium;* and touched thousands through her speaking. She lives in New Jersey with her husband and her dog, Finn.

Connect with Bridget:

➤ visibilityonpurpose.com
➤ bridgetaileen.com
➤ podcasts.apple.com/us/podcast/she-builds-empires/id1546684870
➤ instagram.com/bridgetaileensicsko

Work with Us

Let this section serve as your personal directory for experts in the field who are all eager to guide you to success as an author in the ever-changing publishing industry.

KRYSTAL HILLE

HILLE HOUSE PUBLISHING

If you are a purpose-led entrepreneur, divine feminine leader, coach, consultant, or professional here to make a bigger impact and serve in a deeper way by sharing your wisdom with tens of thousands of readers and potential clients, then one of our programmes might just be right for you. We take you by the hand and provide step-by-step systems and strategies that make the process of writing easy, even if you don't think you're a writer.

My team and I deeply care about our authors, and I have a profound understanding of humanity and the ability to activate and reflect your own essence back to you so that you can capture it more easily on the page. With a sensitivity for cultures (I've lived in four different countries and visited many more), throughout my life experiences I have gained buckets of humility and compassion for the human condition. My high-level systems and professionalism are underpinned by a deeply intuitive awareness and extrasensory abilities.

As a hybrid publisher, my team and I provide all-done-for-you publishing services at a cost to the client, who keeps 100 percent of the copyright and royalties. Our turnaround is much quicker than that of traditional publishing houses, and we award authors sovereignty over their work, plus you don't need a large following to be accepted. We take the headache out of publishing and launching your book so that you can focus on what you do best: sharing your message and working with your clients.

WHAT WE OFFER

➢ *Multiauthor books.* Also known as compilation books or anthologies, multiauthor books offer a great way to dip your toes into publishing to gain confidence in your writing abilities, tap into the communities of other contributors, and meet new friends and collaboration partners. They're also your answer if you lack time but want to profit from the benefits of being a bestselling author quickly. You get to contribute one chapter to a particular theme whilst sharing your personal magic and expertise.

In our containers, we don't just publish books that entertain or educate, but books that have the power to transform both the reader and writer alike. For this purpose, we provide extensive training on intuitive writing for deeper connection, how to choose and create stories strategically, and where to place them in your chapter so that they move the reader into action.

We have created a simple, time-efficient system for our contributors and offer launch strategy training, writing labs, transformational group coaching, and networking circles that have led to many joint ventures between past participants.

➢ *We partner with heads of organisations* that are looking to increase brand awareness by featuring their members in anthologies. They could be not-for-profits or training institutes that want to add value to their students and get a competitive edge whilst providing an additional income stream. We also partner with entrepreneurs who help their clients become more visible in other ways and see a compilation book as a great value-add.

➢ *Solo books.* We've recently started to offer a six-month group container for solo authors writing transformational books. This program provides templates, systems, and writing training for your book, as well as accountability, regular writing labs, feedback, and coaching support for when you get overwhelmed, self-sabotage, or need extra support to work through past wounds that are surfacing through the writing process. If you already have a finished first draft, we also provide *manuscript assessments,* and once your book is edited, we have several publishing packages for you to choose from.

➤ *Writers Temple.* This is our community. It's for people who are not quite ready to write but know they have a book inside them. We meet monthly to explore and worship your creativity, unleash your imagination, inspire you to fall more deeply in love with yourself and your story, and foster your writing skills in a fun way.

➤ *Regular masterclasses.* We all have a stroke of creative writing genius within us. These classes will help you unleash it!

FREE GIFTS

Author Archetype Quiz. If you would like to effortlessly unleash your writing potential so you can captivate readers and leave a lasting impact with your words, I invite you to take my 3-minute Author Archetype quiz. It will help you identify your strengths and provide writing tips to improve on your weaknesses. Plus, wouldn't you want to know whether you are a Watery Mystic or a Fiery Charismatic? Take the quiz here:

➤ krystalhille.org/author-archetype-quiz

Three Keys to Develop a Deeper Connection with Your Reader. This pocket guide is for you if you've ever written something you were sure would create a powerful reaction... but no one responded. Uncover the three keys to deeply connect with your reader, master the art of blending knowledge and emotion for a more profound impact, and claim your Storytelling Success Formula for free. Get your hands on the pocket guide now:

➤ bit.ly/3xUsmlv

Thank you for your vision and leadership. Your ability to create a safe and generative frame and model for creativity and co-collaboration is so very much needed today.

—Keen Nichols,
contributing author of *Inspired Living*

LARISSA SOEHN

NEXT PAGE WELLNESS COACHING

Deciding to seek help to pursue your goals is one of the smartest things you can do for both you and your business.

There are a few ways I can support you with your business goals:

> ➢ Write and publish a book to grow your business
> ➢ Get started on your book
> ➢ Publish your already written manuscript
> ➢ Reach bestseller status with your self-published book
> ➢ Coordinate a collaboration book

Let's look at the programs in more detail.

BOOST YOUR BUSINESS WITH A BOOK

I'm ready to go all in! If you're ready to jump in and get your book out in the world, the *Boost Your Business with a Book* program is perfect for you. In this program, you receive the following:

> ➢ One-on-one coaching for all phases
> ➢ A complete, detailed book outline
> ➢ Guided goal-setting
> ➢ Developmental editing
> ➢ Marketing plan with done-for-you graphics
> ➢ Done-for-you cover and interior design
> ➢ Self-publishing support
> ➢ Promotion of you and your work
> ➢ A published paperback and ebook

I am also pleased to share that my company, Next Page Publishing, Inc., proudly offers literary grants to those with projects that align with our values. We support authors looking to change the world, build their brands, and own their authority. If this sounds like you, I highly encourage you to apply for this prestigious grant.

PAVE THE WAY AND START WRITING TODAY

I'm ready to start but need a bit more time. If you need some more time to get your thoughts straight and organized but still want the one-on-one experience of a hands-on coach, the *Pave the Way and Start Writing Today* program is the choice for you. In this program, you receive the following:

- ➤ One-on-one coaching
- ➤ Detailed publishing training
- ➤ A complete book outline
- ➤ Guided goal-setting
- ➤ Developmental editing of your first three chapters

READY, SET, PUBLISHED

I have a manuscript, but don't know what to do next. If you are ready to move from writing into the next phase of the publishing journey, *Ready, Set, Published* is the place you want to be. In this program, you receive the following:

- ➤ Developmental editing of your entire manuscript
- ➤ Marketing plan with done-for-you graphics
- ➤ Done-for-you cover and interior design
- ➤ Self-publishing support
- ➤ Promotion of you and your work
- ➤ A published paperback and ebook

BESTSELLER BOOT CAMP

I have a published book but want to be a bestseller! This is a very exciting time for self-published authors as we break glass ceilings and claim titles that used to be exclusive to traditionally published authors. In this group program, I guarantee that you will hit bestseller status in at least one category in at least one country, or you get your money back. This program includes the following:

- ➢ Detailed marketing plan
- ➢ Guest blog post and podcast interview
- ➢ Amazon category optimization
- ➢ Done-for-you marketing graphics
- ➢ Long text marketing content
- ➢ Website for marketing with email collection system
- ➢ Minimum of three long text reviews
- ➢ Guaranteed sales

COLLABORATION BOOKS

If you are interested in putting together a collaboration book, I would love to support you on the journey. Please reach out, as my services vary depending on your needs.

If you are interested in working with me, please find all my available resources, including my free guide to getting started on your book today, here:

- ➢ linktr.ee/nextpagepublishing

JAMES WOOSLEY

FREE AGENT PRESS

There's something about writing a book that grants you authority and expertise in the marketplace. But it only works if the book is professionally written and designed.

You don't have to be a great writer to have a great book. All you need is a message you want to share with the world (your audience or target market) and a commitment to developing great content with professional packaging.

At Free Agent Press, we make it easy for speakers, coaches, and authors to publish great books.

You don't need to learn design fundamentals or technical specifications. We'll walk with you through the entire process.

OUR SERVICES INCLUDE THE FOLLOWING:
- Layout and design for print and ebooks
- Print-on-demand distribution and e-commerce
- Content creation and ghostwriting
- Editing and proofreading
- Author coaching
- Audiobook production
- Author and book websites
- A writer's community
- Publishing mastermind programs

Free Agent Press gives you all the benefits of self-publishing without the hard work, and it's much faster than working with a conventional publisher. We offer multiple approaches to fit your needs:

- ➤ Done-for-you, or assisted self-publishing (fee for service and you keep all rights and royalties)
- ➤ Hybrid publishing (we share rights and royalties for a discounted fee)
- ➤ Traditional publishing (we act as your publisher at no cost to you)

Learn more at FreeAgentPress.com and schedule a free consultation (no obligation, no sales pitch).

You don't have to do it yourself. Let's work together to change the world.

PUBLISHING MASTERMIND

Our 12-month mastermind program for coaches, speakers, and authors is the ultimate solution to help you publish your book and grow your business! Our comprehensive program covers everything from outlining and writing your book to design, editing, printing, distribution, sales, and launching.

With interactive community support, monthly group calls, and expert guest speakers, you'll get the guidance and accountability you need to succeed. Plus, our one-on-one coaching ensures you reach your goals and achieve your full potential as an author.

Join our program today and transform your book idea into a professionally designed and published book that elevates your business!

Learn more at FreeAgentPress.com/mastermind.

DR. KRISTINA TICKLER WELSOME

SCAN ME

THE KEY PUBLISHING HOUSE

What is the "key" to getting published? What happens when a bestselling author opens a publishing company? Magic!

Due to my own failures, lessons learned, and experience gained while writing my international bestselling solo book, *LOVE(d): The Key to Unlocking Your True Potential & Living an Authentic Life You Love,* and chapters in numerous multiauthor books, I decided to start my own independent publishing house. As a doctor of physical therapy and a national board-certified health and wellness coach, I provide a supportive space where you are empowered to create a loving relationship with your authentic self, reveal what you really want to say, decide how you want to say it so it's shared in your own voice, and build the confidence to be open and vulnerable with your earned wisdom.

Do you dream of becoming a published author "someday," but don't think you have the time to commit, are afraid you're not a good enough writer, or are bewildered by the publishing process?

The Key Publishing House was founded on the premise that healing people heals the world. Your story matters, and we want to help you share it. I envision a world where each heart and soul that grows, learns, expands, and transforms from its learned experiences has the potential to heal not only us as individuals, but the world at large.

When people feel called to share a story, they often talk themselves out of doing it because they don't know how to write, or they know how to write but they don't know how to call it into creation. That's what I'm here for—to help you figure out how to take the next best step and determine if your path is one of self-publishing; working with an intimate, independent publishing house like The Key Publishing House; or getting an agent and writing a book proposal to submit to traditional publishing houses. You'll need to consider whether you want to be a published author, a bestselling author, or even an international bestselling author!

My favorite is when I get a client who says, "I have a story that needs to be told and I want to share it with the world." Yes! Let's make *you* a published author. I love helping authors connect to their own authentic voice and find the courage to vulnerably share their story. Find out how to become a bestselling author in a multiauthor book or get the support you need to publish your own solo book.

The Key Publishing House can support your dreams with the following:

- One-on-one coaching and book development
- Writers workshops
- Editing
- Proofreading
- Formatting
- Amazon KDP setup
- Printing
- Bestseller campaigns
- Cover design and marketing
- Multiauthor collaboration books
- Mini- or full-length solo books
- Legacy books

Are you ready to rewrite your own authentic story and live a life you love? You can get started by answering the call to write. Hop on a call with me to figure out your own personal path to go from aspiring writer to published author. During this session, I will personally help you understand the options available to you, craft a strategy to reach your goal, answer all of your questions, and walk you through your own strategic plan to publication. I'm here to help make your dreams of becoming a published author come true, however that vision appears to you.

BRIGID HOLDER

THE ART OF GRACE PUBLISHING HOUSE

At The Art of Grace Publishing House, our vision is clear: we assist women to publish their stories to enable others to change their current reality. We want to help you achieve your dreams of becoming a published author. Whether you're a seasoned writer, or you're just starting to explore your passion for writing, we're here to support you every step of the way.

We offer a range of programs tailored to meet your specific needs. Our flagship program is the Bestselling Multiauthor Book Program, which brings together like-minded individuals who want to create a book that will become a bestseller. We take care of everything from the initial planning stages to the editing and design. Together we will market the book. You concentrate on writing your chapter and sharing your own personal journey.

Alternatively, our Launch Your Legacy program is designed for people who want to write and publish a solo book. Whether you've always dreamed of writing your memoir, or you have expert knowledge you want to share with others, we can help you achieve your goals. Through a series of nurturing sessions, as the Book Mumma I will guide you through the writing process, from developing your idea to putting the finishing touches on your final draft.

No matter which program you choose, you can be assured that you will receive the highest level of support from me and our team. We understand that writing a book can be a daunting experience, and we're here to help you every step of the way. Our team is committed to getting to know you on a personal level so that we can understand your unique writing style and help you to achieve your vision.

At The Art of Grace Publishing House, we don't just publish books; we create legacies. Our goal is to help you share your unique voice with the world and leave a lasting impact on the lives of your readers. Whether you want to inspire, educate, or entertain, we have the expertise and passion to help you achieve your goals.

So, what are you waiting for? If you're ready to take the next step on your journey to becoming a published author, then get in touch with us today to learn more about our programs and how we can help you launch your legacy.

➢ brigidholder@gmail.com
➢ brigid-holder.mykajabi.com/multi-author-book-program

K LAFLEUR-ANDERS

SCAN ME

CHESTNUT PUBLISHING HOUSE

If you're interested in telling your story but imposter syndrome won't stop knocking on your mental door, the system of journaling that I've created will help you pause, release, reflect, and reset. I teach my clients how to counter those negative thoughts and feelings through carefully curated writing prompts and discussions. Through expressive journaling, one-on-one guidance, and a supportive group environment, you'll build self-confidence and self-grace and send that imposter packing.

If you're interested in publishing a book but can't seem to clear your mental space, I'm inviting you to take moments to pause, breathe, and focus on *being* through expressive writing. I'm holding space for you. What you have lived and learned is a story worth telling. Not only will it be therapeutic for you, but it will also inspire, encourage, empower, inform, educate, and give hope and light to others. Tap into the courage it takes to be vulnerable so you can discover the endless possibilities of storytelling. If you need support, I am here to help you tell your story and publish without pressure as you create, heal, and grow.

If you desire to tell stories through

- ➤ nonfiction collaboration books,
- ➤ ebooks, eMags, or blogs,
- ➤ nonfiction solo books, or
- ➤ fiction solo books,

I can help you

- ➤ prioritize your well-being to clear your mental space and unlock your creativity,
- ➤ establish a journaling practice to discover your voice and flow,
- ➤ write a book, publish an eMag, or start a blog with clarity and purpose,
- ➤ counter negative thoughts and feelings through creative projects,
- ➤ connect with a community of supportive women writers,
- ➤ unearth emotional, social, physical, and mental weights,
- ➤ build your self-confidence, practice self-grace, and send the imposter packing.

MY COACHING PROCESS

Once you sign up for my group coaching program, you will be invited to join an exclusive community of women writers. Through journaling and various other projects, including collaboration books, we work together to boost our creativity through the connections we make. For six weeks, we focus on building relationships through collaborations, peeling back emotional layers, encouraging physical movement, and practicing deep breathing, among other soul-healing exercises. We dig deep to pull out the story in you that's just waiting to be told.

After the program is over, I won't leave you out there alone. You will still have this community, and you will be able to work on a solo project if that's your desire. The coaching program is designed to help you drop those weights, build self-confidence, and walk with the courage needed to be vulnerable and visible.

If you're interested in telling your story and would like to conquer your fears, email me at info@chestnutbooks.com.

RUTH FAE

FAE BLOOD PUBLICATIONS

Tell stories with me.

Blessed to work with both authors and publishers in two distinct capacities, I stand for silenced voices around the world being healed and heard.

INTUITIVE WRITING COACHING FOR COLLABORATIVE AND SOLO BOOK AUTHORS

In my one-on-one work with authors, writing, coaching, and editing flow together in a safe and nonjudgmental space of co-creation. Storytelling is a beautiful adventure of trust and understanding, as well as gentleness and compassion.

I guide authors to share their story confidently, authentically, and in their own voice. Tapping into your creativity can be daunting, so I work closely with every author at both a practical and energetic level to ensure they are supported and nurtured throughout their transformative journey.

THE POWER OF CO-CREATION

Guidance and support to help you do the following:

- ➤ Release your story from your head and heart
- ➤ Identify and work through your writing blocks
- ➤ Align with your inner magick; connect with yourself and your reader
- ➤ Increase your confidence and understanding of the writing and editing processes

Create a chapter or book that

> ➢ perfectly represents you (and your business),
> ➢ shows your reader how your experience can help, guide, inspire, and encourage them to achieve their desires,
> ➢ clearly shares your message with the Universe,
> ➢ is 100 percent ready to submit to your publisher, and
> ➢ fills your heart with joy!

EDITING FOR INDIE AND HYBRID PUBLISHING HOUSES

As an editor, I sprinkle magick throughout your author's words, using a combination of the following:

> ➢ Developmental/structural editing
> ➢ Line/copyediting
> ➢ Proofreading

Occupying the space between 'storytelling' and 'publishing', my focus is to honour and maintain the integral voice of the collaborative or solo book author, while providing a sacred professional service to the publishing house.

To explore the various options for working with me, visit:

> ➢ ruthfaewriter.com/write-with-me

Or email me:

> ➢ ruth@faebloodpublications.com.au

ERIN R LUND

SUNSHINE EDITORIAL SERVICES & BOOK COACHING

Contact me when...

> ➤ You know you want to write a transformational book, and you are ready to work with a book coach to help you craft a Master Plan, which includes totally clarifying the book's concept and purpose, fully outlining and structuring it, and beginning to draft it with editorial guidance and feedback so you can write your best book.
> ➤ You have completed writing a transformational book and are seeking a developmental editor to assess it and advise you on its clarity, organization, completeness, flow, and marketability so you can best revise your book.
> ➤ You have completed writing and revising a transformational book and are seeking copyediting to best prepare it for publishing.

Those who work with me through my *Master Plan Book Coaching* package indicated above are eligible to continue receiving coaching from me by purchasing my additional coaching offers, which include a *Propose & Pitch* package for writers intending to seek traditional publishing deals and a *Writing Support* package for all writers, regardless of publishing plans, in which I provide regular guidance and editorial feedback as you continue writing your book.

To request my book coaching packages or editing services, visit my website at sunshineeditorialservices.com and fill out my contact form by indicating whether you are a writer or a publisher and whether you are requesting book coaching or editing services, then sharing some rudimentary information about your project.

- ➤ If you are a publisher, I will follow up within 48 hours to request specific information from you about the project you are publishing, then set up a call to see if we will be a good fit for working together.
- ➤ If you are a writer, I will follow up within 48 hours and either provide you with a specific intake form for book coaching or developmental editing, or simply request your manuscript for review if you are requesting copyediting.
- ➤ If you are requesting book coaching, I will review your intake form responses and materials, and if I feel I can help you with your project, I will set up a brief Zoom call with you to see if we are a good fit for working together.
- ➤ If you are requesting developmental editing, I will review your intake responses and materials, and if I feel I can help you with your project, I will offer you a quote.
- ➤ If you are requesting copyediting and I feel your manuscript is ready for this stage of editing, I will offer you a quote.

I look forward to hearing from you!

TERRI TONKIN

CONNECT WITHIN GHOSTWRITING SERVICES

WHAT I OFFER

- ➢ Ghostwriting services: Manuscripts (nonfiction, memoir, lifestyle, well-being, business), blogs, and content
- ➢ Article rewrites
- ➢ Reviews/rewrites (for authors)

MY 15-STEP PROCESS

1. You want to write a book, blog, or content but don't want to do the writing.
2. Connect with me.
3. We have a conversation/discussion to ensure we are a good match.
4. We decide on what work you wish to complete.
5. We decide on the scope of work, word count, timelines, expectations, and costs. Manuscripts are priced at a flat fee per project; blogs, content, and article rewrites are priced per word count.
6. I write out the agreement with all agreed-upon details and forward it along with the first invoice.
7. You sign and return the agreement and payment is processed.
8. I sign and provide a copy of the agreement.
9. I commence writing. If I am completing a manuscript, I write the first chapter and seek feedback.
10. If required, I will amend to ensure I am capturing your voice, passion, and intent. If acceptable, I will proceed with writing.

11. At the midpoint of the manuscript, the second invoice is processed.
12. At the completion of the manuscript, the final invoice is processed.
13. If writing a blog, content, or article rewrite, one invoice is processed.
14. If providing a review or rewrite for an author, one invoice is processed, priced per word count.
15. Upon completion of the manuscript, I will provide referrals to editors, publishers, marketers, etc.

OUTCOME

➢ You will have written blogs, content, and article rewrites to use as you please.
➢ If a manuscript, you decide if/when/how to publish.
➢ If you publish, you become a published author.
➢ All work becomes yours.

Let me help you tell, write, and share your story.

Email: Terri@ConnectWithin.com.au

DRAGONFLY DE LA LUZ

SCAN ME

DRAGONFLY EDITING

I am a highly skilled, multitalented hybrid editor who excels at all facets of editing across all stages of the writing and publishing process. As nerdy as it sounds, it's kinda my thing. I couldn't stop editing if I tried, and I love it so much, I'd never even want to! I'm the one editors hire to edit their own writing. I also edited this book. With me as your editor, you don't have to be a naturally talented writer to sound like one. If you want editing done properly, thoroughly, and with a quick turnaround by a trained, professional with two decades of experience who's also a writer, I'm your girl.

SERVICES OFFERED
- ➢ Developmental editing
- ➢ Line editing/Copyediting
- ➢ Proofreading
- ➢ Ghostwriting
- ➢ Writing assistance
- ➢ Editorial assessments

PUBLISHERS, ACTIVATE ME WHEN...
- ➢ *The writers in your multiauthor book have submitted the best draft of their chapter that they're capable of.* I will step in and do whatever version of editing is required based on the skill of the individual writer, be it developmental editing, copyediting, or even light ghostwriting, as needed.
- ➢ *Your author's manuscript is complete.* I'll do a thorough copyedit wherein I correct any spelling, grammatical, or factual errors; eliminate distractions caused by confusing or awkward

phrasing; catch any errors or typos you may have missed; ensure consistency of style and tone (crucial for multiauthor books); and polish language in a way that connects with and draws in your audience.

➢ *Your author's manuscript is ready to be published.* I will be that final pair of eagle eyes that will proofread your book right before publication to make sure it is free of any typographical or formatting errors, so your finished product looks impeccable and you are taken seriously as a publisher.

WRITERS, ACTIVATE ME WHEN...

➢ *You've just begun your project.* All writing begins with a massive idea dump. I will provide a developmental edit to help you formulate a cohesive structure around your great ideas so they can be crafted into a compelling narrative arc that keeps readers turning the page. Activating me at this stage will reel you in before you veer off course, ensuring you are writing within a solid structure that makes sense from the start and guides your next steps, instead of wasting precious time on pages you'll scrap because you meandered and lost focus.

➢ *You're stuck and need writing assistance.* Are there some sections of your project that you just wish someone else could write for you? This is one of my specialties. I have an uncanny ability to emulate your voice and elevate your writing while capturing the essence of your heart. While I am available to ghostwrite complete projects, I can provide tremendous value by ghostwriting isolated sections as well. Sometimes this is all that's needed to get you unstuck and inspired to move forward with renewed momentum and a solid sense of direction.

➢ *You want an expert opinion on the quality of your writing.* Your mom likes it... Your bestie loves it... But is it any good? It is not only healthy to want an outside perspective on your writing, it's essential to obtain one. Maybe you've looked at the screen for so long you don't know what parts of your story are working or lacking. I will take an objective look and give you an expert editorial assessment on what works and what doesn't, so you can move ahead with confidence.

➤ *Your manuscript is complete: It's time to make your writing shine.* Once everything you want to say is written, I will turn your writing into beautiful, stylistic prose (line editing) that invites the reader to indulge and delight in the pages. After obtaining a clear understanding of the audience you want to reach, I will make your writing sparkle, shine, and speak directly to your ideal reader. In my delicate care, this line/copyediting phase is where good writing blossoms into something more gorgeous than you ever imagined possible.

➤ *Your manuscript is ready for publication.* I'll pull out all the stops to ensure your work is copyedited, proofread, error-free, and polished to perfection. You'll walk away with a meticulously edited manuscript that instantly enhances your credibility and ensures you are taken seriously by readers, agents, and clients alike.

This is A-M-A-Z-I-N-G!!!!! Thank you S-O-O-O much!!!!! Your version is MUCH, MUCH, MUCH better!!!!! As I was reading it, it was very difficult—with only a couple of exceptions—for me to determine which were your edits and which was my original verbiage! You are an E-X-C-E-L-L-E-N-T editor!!!!! WOOOOOW!!!!!

—Maria D.,
Writer

Your edits are AMAZING! 😭 Reading the edited version literally brought me to tears… Thank you! I am so grateful for your amazing contributions on this project. Thank you!

—Nicolette Halladay,
Publisher, Inspired Hearts Publishing

Ready for me to work my magic on your or your client's writing? Let's chat. Email me at dragonflydelaluz@gmail.com.

SERENA SCARLETT

SCARLETT CREATIVE

We offer the following editing services for publishers only:

- ➢ Multiauthor books
- ➢ Solo author books
- ➢ Partnership books
- ➢ Fiction and nonfiction
- ➢ Ebooks

- ➢ Marketing blurbs
- ➢ Website copy
- ➢ Oracle cards
- ➢ Editing and writing courses
- ➢ Special projects

Purchase my affordable *Fixed Fee Publishing Pack* where the price for the service is on the application (based on word count). Read more about my offers here: scarlettcreativ.com

We focus on transforming draft chapters or full manuscripts into polished professional books that you can be proud of.

Being a counsellor/therapist with vast personal and lived experience, I offer the following expertise in the broad inspiration genre:

- ➢ Editing topics on spirituality, traditional wisdom, and personal development/self-help; small business mentoring; coaching; counselling/therapy; life challenges and journeys; helping changemakers; and more.

Existing publisher reviews are available. Simply contact me so I can connect you to the publishing houses personally.

Email me directly at spirit444@gmail.com.

MARY E. GREGORY

AUTHOR AND SPEAKER

I am available for the following opportunities:

- ➤ Media interviews on podcasts, television, print, and online publications
- ➤ Speaking engagements for talks, summits, and workshops
- ➤ Collaborative working projects for books, screenplays, and blogs
- ➤ Content creation through ghostwriting, leading ideation sessions, and providing consulting services

At my core, I am an unapologetic forgiver, sympathizer of the human condition, and thoughtful creator. I enjoy delivering work that is engaging and anchored in vulnerability and authenticity.

If you have a project that is not listed above, please contact me so we can discuss it.

KRISTINA CONATSER

CAPTURED BY KC DESIGNS

At Captured by KC Designs, we provide graphic design, print, and digital design services for entrepreneurs, coaches, authors, startups, and small to medium-sized businesses. Whether you are a startup looking to build your brand or an existing business looking to revamp or rebrand; whether you're publishing a book or want to create an online presence—we've got you covered!

We have a passion for artistic expression that captures the attention of your intended audience. You have an idea; we are the visual storytellers who can conceptualize that idea and bring it into reality.

OUR PROCESS

Envision. You envision the message you want to send to your audience. We help you to zero in on that message with a deep dive discovery session into your brand, your mission, your target audience, and your goals.

Conceptualize. We work together every step of the way to map out and pinpoint the visual elements of your idea through concepts in order to bring your vision to life.

Realize. We put all the approved visual elements together and add the finishing touches to create your finalized creative design. Your vision... realized.

You've envisioned an idea for your business. Let's work together to conceptualize and realize it through creative design.

OUR SERVICES

As a wearer of many hats and doer of many things, book cover design just wasn't enough for this graphic designer. Captured by KC Design also provides services in various other digital and print media. Some of these services include, but are not limited to, branding design, digital and print marketing design, logo design, children's book cover design and formatting, wedding and party stationery design, and so much more.

We succeed when our clients succeed. We work directly with our clients every step of the way to provide graphic design, print, and web design that is custom-tailored to their vision. The mission is to work with businesses large and small to help envision, conceptualize, and realize their brands and help them achieve their goals.

Are you ready to take the next step in your business or dream venture? How can we help you bring your vision to life?

Get in touch with us at capturedbykcdesigns.com. We can't wait to work with you! Let's create something amazing together.

Scan the QR code above to download your FREE fillable Discovery Sheet, which guides you through some of the intricate questions that will help you shape your brand and brand identity.

MEAGAN CAESAR

MEAG E CAESAR DESIGNS

Contact me when...

- ➤ You need support to launch your book with ease.
- ➤ You want your book and message to be instantly recognisable and memorable.
- ➤ You understand the importance of consistently connecting with your potential readers.
- ➤ Branding, marketing, and graphic design are *not* your thing, and you know the value of outsourcing.
- ➤ You're ready to ditch the overwhelm or take some tasks off your to-do list by implementing simple, supportive systems for your book launch or business.

At the foundational level, I create beautiful graphics and videos that allow you to market with ease. In addition, I create individualised marketing content, launch strategy guides, project management hubs for publishers, multiauthor collaboration spaces, systems to eliminate overwhelm and keep you on track, and branding to bring your book to life.

All of this comes with my unique educational approach, which supports anyone at any experience level to go all-in to launch their book and leverage the incredible achievement that is becoming an author.

So, what are the key steps when I brand your book?

Step 1. I learn all about the vibe and message of your book, its core purpose, as well as what you hope to receive from working with me. Knowing what will create the most impact for you, the best way I can support you, and what you need to launch your book with ease allows me to tailor my offers to suit your requirements.

Step 2. Through my style guide template, I gather information on the cover (or *for* the cover, if I'm designing it for you), colour palette, fonts, and other visuals of your book, your target audience, and you as the author or publisher.

Step 3. I then craft the marketing graphics and videos in Canva that allow you to share your vision and message authentically and consistently, so that you're reaching your aligned audience. I capture the essence of both you and your book so that the right audience connects with your writing. If you've chosen to include any of my systems services, then your graphics will be accompanied by documents and templates that outline everything in an easy-to-implement format. But even my basic services come with tips and guidance to help you make the most of what I've designed for you.

Step 4. I support and cheer you on throughout the process, including a year down the track when you're celebrating your bookiversary and reflecting on how far you've come since launching your book—I'm all about legacy and longevity! I'm available for questions, I can make tweaks and changes if something isn't working for you, and I ensure you feel confident using everything I've set up. My years of experience as a teacher and my knowledge of how to differentiate and scaffold for different ability levels give me a unique approach. I not only deliver professional, high-quality, beautiful products, I also ensure you have tips, instructions, and further options to support you, no matter your level of experience or technical knowledge.

Does this sound like something that could work for you? Get in touch! Connect with me through my socials or head to my website to check out some of the resources, tips, and freebies. When you're ready to work with me, submit an enquiry through the form on my website, and we can get started on branding your book.

CAROLYN CHOATE

FINANCIALLY FREE AUTHOR

I help authors with all the backend tech that is the foundation of their marketing. It starts with a **funnel-mapping strategy session** where we can talk through the exact right funnel structure for you (because there is no such thing as a one-size-fits-all funnel!).

Once you have your funnel map, you can hire me to create it all for you in one week with a *Funnel by Friday* or you can opt to do it yourself (and I've got a DIY course to help guide you through that too).

Finally, after you set up a funnel, you need to bring people to it. *Website Traffic School* is an online membership that teaches the four pillars of traffic with weekly lessons, challenges, accountability threads, and guest experts.

Join me for a *free live class* hosted on Zoom where I'll walk you through how a sales funnel is really a cobblestone path to your doorstep and you can ask your questions on the spot.

Register here: financiallyfreeauthor.com/liveclass

NICOLETTE HALLADAY

SCAN ME

INSPIRED HEARTS PUBLISHING

Writing a book can be an intimidating and daunting task. You have a story to tell, and you've always wanted to share your work with the world, but you just don't know how to get started. Inspired Hearts Publishing is a full-service self-publishing provider, supporting authors in publishing solo and multiauthor books.

Publishing a book instantly creates credibility for you as an expert in your industry. Plus, when you have a published book under your belt, it becomes much easier to land speaking gigs or get interviewed by top media outlets. In addition, publishing a book can help open new doors and opportunities you never thought possible.

If you're ready to take your career or business to the next level, then publishing a book is definitely something you should consider. And with our help, it's easier than ever to get published.

Below are the opportunities available to partner with Inspired Hearts Publishing.

LIGHT-BEARERS BOOK COLLECTIVE COMMUNITY

This group is for thought leaders, healers, spiritual mentors, and transformational coaches interested in writing and publishing a solo book inside a community. Here is what's included:

- ➤ Support and guidance on writing your 25,000 – 40,000-word manuscript

- ➤ Professional cover design and interior formatting for the digital and paperback releases of your book
- ➤ Become a bestselling author with our live launch support and bestseller book launch campaign
- ➤ Weekly live group calls via Zoom for guidance on writing your manuscript, promoting your book while you write, and growing your business in the process
- ➤ Access to the Light-Bearers Book Collective private Facebook group.

PUBLISHING SOLO AUTHOR BOOKS

Writing a solo book is an amazing accomplishment. Publishing it is the next step! Our team of experts can help you design an eye-catching cover, edit and format your book for publication, create an Amazon bestselling strategy that will boost visibility, and provide guidance for launching your work into the world. Plus, we'll promote your title like crazy to make sure as many people as possible know about it!

PUBLISHING MULTIAUTHOR BOOKS

Writing a solo book requires a big time and financial commitment that not everyone is ready for. This is where our multiauthor book opportunity comes in. You contribute a chapter and share your story or expertise in a book around a certain theme. Becoming a published author becomes easy with our tools, resources, and guidance.

Plus, as an added bonus, we have supportive community authors who are there for each other on the journey. It's an incredibly exciting and healing experience that will lead to success (and publication!). So, what are you waiting for? It's time to start writing.

BRIDGET SICSKO

SCAN ME

VISIBILITY ON PURPOSE

If visibility and getting more eyes on your business are in your future, let's talk!

I support impact-driven business owners in their efforts to amplify their message beyond social media through books, podcasts, speaking, and media exposure.

What do I mean by "impact-driven"?

I work with brands that feel deeply connected to the mission of their work. They know their business is here to make a difference in people's lives.

Many of my clients work in the healing arts, transformational, business strategy, sustainability, and eco-conscious realms. They are here to make lots of money while also serving humanity.

Think of it like this. You can call me when...

> ➤ Your brand needs a *messaging revamp* (because your target market has changed, you've pivoted your business, or you are offering a new service).
> ➤ You desire *more eyes* on your brand and your business.
> ➤ You want to speak on *podcasts* and *stages*, but you're not sure what you would speak about.
> ➤ You want to learn how to get *press* and *media exposure* for your brand, but you're not ready to hire a publicist yet.

➢ You want a master training or workshop for your community on topics related to storytelling, press and media, amplifying your message, or the spiritual and practical steps towards media exposure.

Want support from a community of like-minded business owners?

Visibility on Purpose is the media training school that my business partner, Lydia Bagarozza, and I co-founded in 2023. We teach impact-driven business owners how to build their thought leadership platform and land top-tier media without hiring a publicist. We liken Visibility on Purpose to the Hogwarts of media training, being that we blend the spiritual and practical steps to gain massive brand recognition and media exposure.

Our clients have gotten themselves featured in outlets like *AskMen, Girlboss, Medium, Elpha, Bustle,* and more.

Learn more about Visibility on Purpose at visibilityonpurpose.com.

Get Published: Industry Experts Share Their Secrets
is a valuable resource for anyone looking to
break into the publishing industry. The book is a
collection of insights and tips from experienced
authors, editors, book coaches, publishers, and
marketing experts sharing their knowledge and
expertise on the process of getting published.

To delve deeper into the wealth of knowledge
contained within these pages, we have launched an
Author Interview Series featuring the co-authors
of the book. In this series, readers can gain further
insights and advice on the publishing industry
from the experts themselves.

Join us on YouTube as we explore the wisdom and
experience of these industry leaders in the
Get Published: Industry Experts Share Their Secrets
Author Interview Series.

SCAN ME